TASTE AND TALE NATIONAL PARKS EAST

A COLLECTION OF DELICIOUS RECIPES, FUN FACTS AND ENTERTAINING TALES

WRITTEN AND EDITED BY
P. ANN PIEROWAY

COVER AND ILLUSTRATIONS BY
ERIN SWEENEY

DESIGNED BY
ERIN SWEENEY

BASS POND PRESS
SPRINGFIELD, MA

Taste and Tales of our National Parks East

Published by
Bass Pond Press
Springfield, MA 01129, U.S.A.
info@tasteandtales.com

Copyright © 2019 by P. Ann Pieroway

Cover and Illustrations Copyright © 2019 by Erin Sweeney
Erin Sweeney Design
erin@erinsweeneydesign.com

Designed by Erin Sweeney

Library of Congress Cataloging-in-Publication Data
Pieroway, P. Ann
Taste and Tales of our National Parks East... / P. Ann Pieroway
Cover and Illustrations by Erin Sweeney
ISBN 978-0-9755794-4-2
Printed in Massachusetts • First Printing 2019

Other Books By P. Ann Pieroway
Taste and Tales of Massachusetts
Taste and Tales of Coastal New England
Taste and Tales of Cape Cod
Taste and Tales of New York
A taste of cranberries…and some tales, too
A taste of apples…and some tales, too
A taste of lobsters…and some tales, too

All rights reserved. No portion of the contents of this book may be reproduced or transmitted in any form or by any means without prior written permission of the publisher.

MISSION STATEMENT OF NATIONAL PARKS SERVICE

The National Park Service preserves unimpaired the natural and cultural resources and values of the National Park System for the enjoyment, education, and inspiration of this and future generations. The Park Service cooperates with partners to extend the benefits of natural and cultural resource conservation and outdoor recreation throughout this country and the world.

DEDICATION

More than 20,000 strong, the uncommon men and women of the National Park Service share a common trait: a passion for caring for the nation's special places and sharing their stories. This book is dedicated to those many employees of the National Park Service who work hard to maintain our parks. It is also dedicated to the many organizations such as the Friends of the Cape Cod Seashore, Shenandoah National Park Trust, Statue of Liberty-Ellis Island Foundation and the National Parks Foundation who work tirelessly to raise funds for projects in the various parks.

TABLE OF CONTENTS

Appetizers and Beverages..1

Breakfast and Brunch..19

Soup and Salad..41

Entrées..61

Desserts..87

Preserves and More..107

Vegetables and Side Dishes...119

Recipe Index...129

Order Form...135

FALL IN GREAT SMOKEY NATIONAL PARK	MT. RUSHMORE NATIONAL MEMORIAL
GETTYSBURG NATIONAL MILITARY PARK	LIGHTHOUSE CAPE HATTERAS NATIONAL SEASHORE

FRONT COVER

THE EVERGLADES NATIONAL PARK	NIAGARA FALLS NATIONAL HERITAGE AREA
VIEW FROM CADILLAC MOUNTAIN ARCADIA NATIONAL PARK PHOTO BY STEVEN BART	NATIONAL ZOO AT ROCK CREEK PARK

BACK COVER

RIVER OF GRASS

ww.nps.gov/ever/index.htm

The Everglades National Park was established in 1947 to conserve the natural landscape and prevent further degradation of its land, plants, and animals. At one time the River of Grass covered 11,000 square miles from the Kissimmee River to Lake Okeechobee and southward over low-lying lands to the estuaries of Biscayne Bay, the Ten Thousand Islands, and Florida Bay. For thousands of years this intricate system of ponds, sloughs, sawgrass marshes, hardwood hammock, and forested uplands created a finely balanced ecosystem that formed the biological infrastructure for the southern half of the state. However, developers and farmers couldn't wait to start changing the Everglades. As the damage of the ecosystem became evident, conservationists, scientists, and other advocates, came together to conserve the natural landscape and prevent further degradation of its land, plants, and animals.

Appetizers and Beverages

THE EVERGLADES

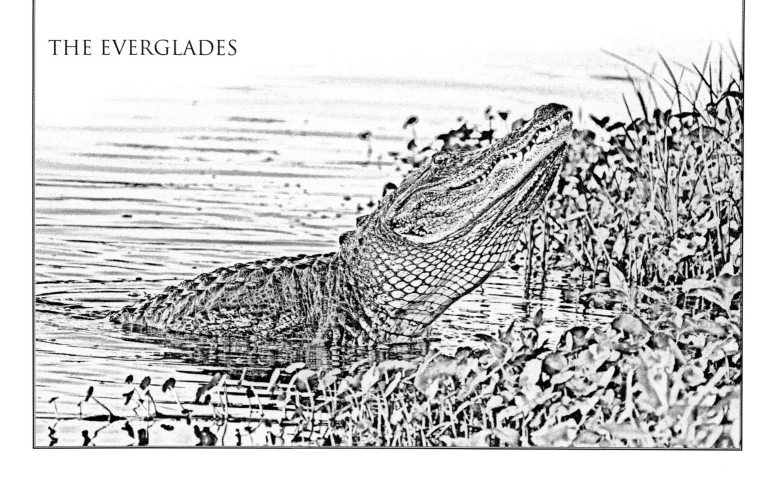

CAPE COD NATIONAL SEASHORE

For once our tax dollars were put to good use. In 1961, the federal government purchased lands that make up the Cape Cod National Seashore Park. The park stretches from Chatham to Race Point in Provincetown and covers 43,607 acres. This was the first time that a national park was created out of privately owned rather than government-owned land. The federal government took by eminent domain about 100 cottages built after 1959. They bought the properties and granted the owners a 25-year lease to rent the cottages at fair market value. Some 600 private homes and a handful of businesses lie within the bounds of the National Seashore, creating a curious melding of private and public spaces. For once some of the glorious beaches and dunes in the World won out over condos.

BAKED CRAB, LOBSTER AND ARTICHOKE DIP

www.marconibeachrestaurant.net

2 (8 ounce) packages cream cheese, softened
4 ounces lobster meat, chopped
4 ounces crab meat, chopped
½ cup Mozzarella cheese
¼ cup grated Parmesan cheese
1 (8 ounce) can artichoke hearts (NOT marinated), drained and chopped
1 tablespoon Old Bay® seasoning
2 tablespoons chopped fresh garlic
1 teaspoon Worcestershire® sauce
2 tablespoons finely chopped scallions juice of one lemon

1. Preheat oven to 350 degrees.
2. Place all ingredients in bowl and mix until combined. Spread in 10" oven safe or microwave safe shallow dish or pie pan.
3. Bake in preheated oven for 10 to 12 minutes or until bubbly.
4. Serve with toasted pita chips or hearty crackers.

Serves 4-6

CHEVRE WITH HERBS DE PROVENCE

1 small log of soft chevre
1 large garlic clove, crushed and chopped
8 ounces cream cheese, softened
2 tablespoons Herbs de Provence

1. Mix all ingredients together.
2. Serve on crackers or bread.

Cook's Notes: Herbs de Provence is made of chopped lavender flowers, rosemary, savory, marjoram, oregano and fennel fronds or seeds.

HOT OYSTER SPINACH DIP

2 cans oysters
2 (10-ounce) packages frozen chopped spinach
1½ cups Italian bread crumbs
1 tablespoon garlic powder
fine sea salt to taste
freshly ground black pepper to taste
pinch tarragon

1. Drain oysters and chop.
2. Cook spinach; drain.
3. Mix with remaining ingredients; heat thoroughly.
4. Serve in chafing dish with fresh vegetables or crackers.

Serves 20

WALKING NOT DRIVING

The National Trails System (60,000 miles) is larger than the Interstate Highway System (46,876 miles) in length and includes 11 National Scenic Trails, 19 National Historic Trails and more than 1,300 National Recreation Trails (including 21 National Water Trails) in all 50 states. What you say is a National Water Trail? The Water Trails Systems have been established to protect and restore America's rivers, shorelines, and waterways and conserve natural areas along waterways. In 2018, the trail system celebrated their 50th anniversary. So whether it is the famous 2,180 miles long Appalachian Trail which begins in Georgia and ends in Maine, covering 14 states along the way or the National Historic Trail from Selma to Montgomery in Alabama there is something for everyone.

TAPENADE DIP

½ cup imported black olives, pitted
¼ cup imported green olives, pitted
4 anchovy fillets
1 garlic clove
2 tablespoons capers, thoroughly drained
2 tablespoons oil-packed tuna, drained
1 tablespoon lemon juice
1 cup fresh basil leaves, rinsed and patted dry, or more to taste
¼ cup quality olive oil
¼ cup mayonnaise

1. Combine black and green olives, anchovy fillets, garlic, capers, tuna, lemon juice and basil in the bowl of a food processor fitted with a steel blade. Process until smooth.
2. With the motor still running, dribble in the oil to make a thick, fluffy sauce. For a lighter sauce, ideal for raw vegetables, blend in the mayonnaise.
3. Taste and correct seasoning. Scrape dip into a bowl and cover. Refrigerate until ready to serve. Serve with crackers. Tapenade will keep refrigerated for 1 week.

Yields: about 1½ cups

Cook's Note: I first had this delicious dip at a friend's house in London. Blair was a wonderful cook and could produce the most amazing meals in her little kitchen on the Grand Canal.

REUBEN DIP

½ pound diced corned beef
1 package (8 ounce) cream cheese, softened
1 cup shredded Swiss cheese
1 cup sauerkraut, drained well
½ cup sour cream
1 tablespoon ketchup
2 teaspoons spicy brown mustard
rye crackers or bread

1. Heat oven to 350 degrees. Grease a 1-quart casserole dish.
2. In a medium size bowl, mix corned beef, cream cheese, Swiss cheese, sauerkraut, sour cream, ketchup and mustard. Spoon into the prepared casserole dish.
3. Bake for 30 minutes, until hot and bubbly. Serve warm with rye crackers or bread.

Yields: 4 cups

"The national parks...are an American idea; it is one thing we have that has not been imported."
J. Horace McFarland 1916

SMOKED MULLET DIP

1½ packages (12 ounce) cream cheese, softened
2 tablespoons mayonnaise
¾ cup smoked mullet, finely chopped
2 tablespoons milk
1 tablespoon onion, finely chopped
2 tablespoons pimiento, chopped

1. Combine all ingredients.
2. Chill.
3. Serve with crackers or chips.

Yields: 1 cup

HOW LONG IS A LONG TIME AGO?

Russell Cave is an archaeological site with one of the most complete records of prehistoric cultures in the Southeast. Thousands of years ago a portion of Russell Cave's entrance collapsed, creating a shelter that, for more than 10,000 years, was home to prehistoric peoples. Today it provides clues to the daily lifeways of early North American inhabitants dating from 10,000 B.C. to 1650 A.D. The Park represents the evolving stages of civilization in southeastern America before European contact, Archeologists have established a general cultural sequence: Paleo, Archaic, Woodland, Mississippian.

SHRIMP BUTTER TOASTS

1½ sticks (¾ cup) unsalted butter, softened
1 pound medium shrimp in shell (31 to 35 per pound), peeled and deveined
1 teaspoon fine sea salt
½ teaspoon freshly ground black pepper
¼ cup minced onion
2½ teaspoons fresh lemon juice
⅛ teaspoon cayenne pepper
10 slices firm white sandwich bread, crustless, cut in 4 triangles
3 tablespoons unsalted butter, melted
whole shrimp for garnish

1. To make shrimp butter, heat 2 tablespoons butter in a 10-inch heavy skillet over moderately high heat until foam subsides, then sauté shrimp with salt and black pepper, stirring, until just cooked through, 1½ to 2 minutes. Transfer shrimp with a slotted spoon to a food processor, reserving skillet (do not clean).
2. Cook onion in 1 tablespoon butter in skillet over moderately low heat, stirring occasionally, softened, 2 to 3 minutes. Scrape onions into processor and cool mixture to room temperature, about 15 minutes.
3. Add lemon juice, cayenne, and remaining 9 tablespoons butter and pulse until shrimp are finely chopped. Pack shrimp butter into a 2-cup ramekin or serving bowl and chill, its surface covered with plastic wrap, at least 6 hours (to allow flavors to develop). Bring to room temperature 45 minutes before serving.
4. To make toast points put oven rack in upper third of oven and preheat oven to 400 degrees. Brush 1 side of bread triangles lightly with melted butter and toast, buttered sides up, in a large shallow baking pan until golden around edges, 6 to 8 minutes. Transfer to a rack to cool. Serve toast points with shrimp butter.

Makes 40 toast points

Cook's Note: Shrimp butter can be chilled up to 2 days. Do not over process shrimp, you want a textured butter and not a paste. Can also be served with benne crackers.

Adapted from Gourmet, April 2007

CRANBERRY BRIE

⅓ cup crushed whole cranberry sauce
2 tablespoons packed brown sugar
¼ teaspoon rum
⅛ teaspoon nutmeg, grated
1 (8-ounce) Brie cheese
2 tablespoons pecans, chopped

1. Preheat oven to 500 degrees.
2. Combine cranberry sauce, brown sugar, rum and nutmeg.
3. Cut off the top rind of cheese, leaving a rim. Top the Brie with the cranberry mixture and sprinkle with chopped pecans.
4. Bake for 4 to 5 minutes. Serve hot with crackers.

Serves 8 - 10

WHAT HAPPENED ON THE TRAIL OF TEARS?
www.nps.gov/trte

In the year 1838, 16,000 Native Americans were marched over 1,200 miles of rugged land. Over 4,000 of these Indians died of disease, famine, and warfare. The Indian tribe was the Cherokee and we called this event the Trail of Tears. Why were the Cherokees and four other civilized tribes (Chickasaws, Choctaws, Creeks, and Seminoles) of the Southeastern United States moved to the Indian Territory under the Indian Removal Act of 1830 signed by U.S. president Andrew Jackson? Good ole American greed. The Act allowed the government to move any Indians who lived east of the Mississippi River to territory west of the River. White settlers in the east wanted their land to grown cotton and other crops. Gold was also found on land owned by the Cherokees. Georgia held lotteries to give Cherokee land and gold rights to whites. Cherokees were not allowed to conduct tribal business, make contracts, testify in courts against whites, or mine for gold. Over one-fifth of the Cherokee nation died during the force march from disease, drought, and starvation. In 1839, with John Ross as Chief, they established their capital at Tahlequah, Oklahoma where the tribal headquarters remain today.

SAVING THE BAY

The Chesapeake Bay is the nation's largest estuary and one of the most biologically diverse estuaries in the world and is recognized as a national treasure. The six state, (Delaware, Maryland, New York, Pennsylvania, Virginia and West Virginia—and the entire District of Columbia), 64,000 square-mile watershed is home to more than 18 million people and over 3,000 species of plants and animals. Humans have occupied the Chesapeake Bay area for at least 12,000 years. No one knows when the first humans arrived, but archeologists have found evidence of Paleoindians from 11,500 years ago. European explorers first arrived in the 1500s, and European colonies began to take hold following the founding of Jamestown in 1607. With the increase in population came landscape changes that continue today. The Bay has suffered since colonists began cutting down trees and plowing fields that led to erosion of the soil into the rivers feeding into the Bay. The increasing population growth from about 15,000 in 1500s to 18 million today has put an increasing stress on the resources of the Bay. For foodies, the Bay is well known for soft shell blue crabs and oysters. Because so many of the properties of the NPS fall within the watershed, they work with a variety of agencies to Save the Bay!

SHRIMP DIP

1 pint sour cream
¾ cup chili sauce
1 package onion soup mix
2 cans small shrimp
3 tablespoons horseradish
Tabasco Sauce®, few drops

1. Mix all ingredients and mix well.
2. Serve with crackers or shrimp

Yields: 2 cups

CRABMEAT STUFFED MUSHROOM CAPS

½ pound fresh lump or backfin crabmeat
12 extra large white mushrooms, cleaned with brush or damp paper towel
¼ cup seasoned bread crumbs
1 large garlic clove, minced
¼ cup flat-leaf Italian parsley, chopped
¼ cup fresh Parmesan or Pecorino Romano cheese, grated
½ cup dry sherry wine
¼ cup heavy cream
2 tablespoons almonds, lightly toasted, chopped
fine sea salt to taste
freshly ground black pepper to taste
watercress and lemon wedges for garnish

1. Preheat oven to 300 degrees.
2. Place the crabmeat in a strainer to drain off excess liquid and pick through to remove bits of shell.
3. Remove the stems from the mushrooms leaving only the caps and chop the stems.
4. In a medium bowl, combine the chopped stems, breadcrumbs, garlic, parsley, cheese, sherry, cream and season with salt and pepper. Mix the ingredients lightly, to avoid shredding the crabmeat. Spoon the stuffing into the mushroom caps and sprinkle with chopped almonds.
5. Place the stuffed mushrooms caps on a non-stick baking sheet. Bake for 10-12 minutes until lightly browned.

Serves 6

9 MOST VISITED "NATIONAL PARKS" IN 2018

1. Blue Ridge Parkway
14,690,418
2. Great Smoky Mountains National Park
11,421,200
3. Gateway National Recreation Area
9,243,305
4. Lincoln Memorial
7,804,683
5. George Washington Memorial Parkway
7,288,623
6. Natchez Trace Parkway
6,362,439
7. Vietnam Memorial
4,719,148
8. Cape Cod National Seashore
3,926,462
9. Acadia National Park
3,537,575

Appetizers & Beverages

WHO WERE THE TUSKEGEE AIRMAN?

www.nps.gov/tuai

The Tuskegee Airman were the first African-American aviator in the U.S. Army Air Corp (AAC), the precursor to the U.S. Air Force. In the early 1940s racial segregation ruled in both the military and the country. At that time there were only 2 black officers in the military. In September 1940, President Franklin Roosevelt responded to lobbying from black newpapers and the NAACP, that the AAC would begin training black pilots at Moton Field. Overall, the program at the Tuskegee Institute trained 932 airmen, but only 355 would ever serve as active pilots. In the last two years of WWII, the Tuskegee Airman flew more than 15,000 sorties and sixty-six lost their lives during combat. Overall, the Airman earned more than 150 Distinguished Flying Crosses. Their success changed the military forever and helped end segregation.

COCONUT SHRIMP WITH MUSTARD SAUCE

1½ pounds unpeeled, large raw shrimp
vegetable cooking spray
2 egg whites
¼ cup cornstarch
1 tablespoon Caribbean jerk seasoning
1 cup sweetened flaked coconut
1 cup panko breadcrumbs
Mustard Sauce (page 116)

1. Preheat oven to 425 degrees. Peel shrimp, leaving tails on; devein, if desired.
2. Place a wire rack coated with cooking spray in a 15 x 10-inch jelly-roll pan.
3. Whisk egg whites just until foamy.
4. Stir together cornstarch and jerk seasoning in a shallow dish. Stir together coconut, breadcrumbs, and paprika in another shallow dish.
5. Dredge shrimp, 1 at a time, in cornstarch mixture; dip in egg whites, and dredge in coconut mixture, pressing gently with fingers. Lightly coat shrimp on each side with cooking spray; arrange shrimp on wire rack.
6. Bake for 10 to 12 minutes or just until shrimp turn pink, turning once after 8 minutes.

Serves 4

HOT MUSHROOM TURNOVERS

1 (8-ounce) package cream cheese, softened
1½ cups unbleached all-purpose flour
½ cup butter, softened
3 tablespoons butter
½ pound mushrooms, minced
1 large onion, minced
¼ cup sour cream
1 teaspoon fine sea salt
¼ teaspoon dried thyme
2 tablespoons flour
1 egg, beaten

1. In a large bowl, beat cream cheese, flour and butter on medium speed until smooth; shape into a ball. Wrap in a cellophane wrap and refrigerate for 1 hour.
2. In a skillet, melt butter and sauté onion and mushrooms until tender, stirring occasionally. Stir in sour cream, salt, thyme and flour; set aside.
3. On a floured surface, roll out half the dough ⅛-inch thick with floured rolling pin. With floured 2¾-inch round cookie cutter, cut out as many circles as possible. Repeat with other half dough.
4. Preheat oven to 450 degrees.
5. Onto ½ of each dough piece, place a teaspoon of mushroom mixture. Brush edge of circle with beaten egg; fold dough over filling. With fork, firmly press edges together to seal; prick tops.
6. Place turnovers on ungreased cookie sheet; brush with remaining egg. Bake 12 to 14 minutes until golden brown.

Cook's Note: These are wonderful frozen. When finished step 5, simply place in a sealed plastic bag and place in freezer. When ready to use, place on cookie sheet and bake.

WALK IN BIG FOOT'S STEPS

Who could imagine a crocodile fossil in Wisconsin? Yes, but long before the Ice Age when creatures who were used to living in warm shallow seas that covered the state. Not only were crocodile fossils found but so were bi-valve mollusks (clams), gastropod mollusks (snails), and even coral. A glacier then covered the land and the many lakes, river valleys, the hills and ridges left behind are the best evidence that mammoths once walked these hills. The idea of preserving the fossils began in 1920 and was spearheaded by Ray Zillmer. Work on the trail itself was begun by volunteers in the 1950's and in 1958, Zillmer founded the Ice Age Park & Trail Foundation (now known as the Ice Age Trail Alliance) to begin efforts to establish a national park in Wisconsin. In 1980, the National Park Service established the 1,200 mile Ice Age National Scenic Trail.

FIVE WOMEN WHO CHANGED THE WORLD

In 1848 five women met at Wesleyan Chapel in Seneca Falls, New York and the world has never been the same. Elizabeth Cody Stanton, Jane Hunt, Lucretia Mott, Martha Coffin Wright and Mary Ann McClintock met to organize the first women's rights convention that brought about 100 women together and the Suffrage Movement was born. Historians believe that Stanton was the driving force behind the meeting and for the next 50 years she played a leadership role in the women's rights movement. Elizabeth Cady Stanton died in 1902, and like Anthony and Gage, did not live to see women's suffrage in the United States. She is nonetheless regarded as one of the true major forces in the drive toward equal rights for women in the United States and throughout the world.

SPINACH CHEESE SQUARES

4 tablespoons butter
3 eggs
1 cup flour
1 cup milk
1 teaspoon fine sea salt
1 teaspoon baking powder
1 pound sharp Cheddar cheese, grated
2 packages chopped spinach, thawed & drained

1. Preheat oven to 350 degrees.
2. In a 9 x 13 x 2-inch pan, melt the butter in the oven; remove.
3. In a large bowl, beat the eggs, add flour, milk, salt, and baking powder; mix well. Add cheese and spinach and blend.
4. Pour into buttered pan and bake for 35 minutes. Remove and cool 10 minutes to set. Cut into bite-size squares.

Makes 32 squares

Cook's Note: These can be frozen by putting squares on cookie sheet; place in the freezer and freeze solid. Remove to a plastic bag and store in freezer. Serve by heating squares for 12 minutes at 325 degrees.

SWEDISH MEATBALLS

2 tablespoons butter
⅓ cup onion, minced
1 egg
½ cup milk
½ cup fresh bread crumbs
1¼ teaspoons fine sea salt
2 teaspoons granulated sugar
pinch allspice
pinch nutmeg
1 pound ground chuck (or top round)
¼ pound ground pork
2 tablespoons butter
3 tablespoons unbleached all-purpose flour
1 teaspoon granulated sugar
¾ cup light cream
1 cup water

1. In two tablespoons hot butter in large skillet, sauté onion until golden.
2. In a large mixing bowl, beat egg; add milk and crumbs. Let stand 5 minutes.
3. Add salt, sugar, allspice, nutmeg, meats and onions. Blend well with fork.
4. In the same skillet, heat another two tablespoons butter. Shape meat mixture into ½- to ¾-inch balls. Drop in skillet. Brown well on all sides. Remove to warm casserole.
5. Into fat left in skillet, stir flour, sugar, salt and pepper. Slowly add water, cream and stir until thickened.

Makes about 5 dozen

SAUSAGE STUFFED MUSHROOMS

1½ pounds mushrooms
½ pound Italian sausage
½ cup shredded mozzarella cheese
¼ cup seasoned bread crumbs
parsley

1. Preheat oven to 450 degrees.
2. Remove mushroom stems and chop; set aside.
3. In skillet, over medium heat, cook sausage until well browned. Remove with slotted spoon and drain meat on paper towels. Remove all but about 2 tablespoons drippings from skillet.
4. In hot drippings, over medium heat, cook stems until tender (about 10 minutes); stir frequently. Remove skillet from heat and stir in sausage, cheese and crumbs. Fill caps with mixture.
5. Place in 15½ x 10½-inch pan.
6. Bake 15 minutes. Garnish with parsley.

Serves 12–15

SAINT GAUDENS SCULPTOR TO THE WORLD

www.nps.gov/saga

Saint-Gaudens National Historic Park in Cornish, New Hampshire is a monument to one of the World's greatest sculptor. One of his most impressive pieces is located on the Commons in Boston. It is entitled the "Shaw Memorial" named after Robert Gould Shaw, who was a Colonel and Commander of the first all-black regiment in the Northeast. He encouraged his men to refuse their pay until it was equal to those of white soldiers. Another beautiful sculpture is of General William Tecumseh Sherman at Grand Army Plaza in New York City. Fortunately his many sculptors will exist for future generations.

RASPBERRY LEMONADE COOLER

Annabelle's Ice Cream · Portsmouth, NH

www.annabellesicecream.com

2 tablespoons granulated sugar
2½ cups water
juice of 2 lemons
1 pint red raspberry sorbet
lemon slices
fresh raspberries

1. Combine sugar, water and lemon juice in a pitcher; stir well.
2. In a blender, mix the lemonade and raspberry sorbet; mix until blended.
3. Pour into glasses and garnish with lemon slices and fresh raspberries.
4. Serve immediately

Serves 4

MOJITO

2 sprigs mint
juice of 3 Key Limes
1 teaspoon granulated sugar
1½ ounces white rum
soda water
cracked ice

1. Place 1 sprig of mint, juice, and granulated sugar into a 10-ounce glass. Blend with a long spoon crushing leaves to extract mint flavor.
2. Add white rum, then soda water to top; stir well.
3. Add second sprig of mint; stir again.
4. Serve cold.

Serves 1

> "National parks are the best idea we ever had. Absolutely American, absolutely democratic, they reflect us at our best rather than our worst."
> Wallace Stegner, 1983

NATIONAL PARK SERVICE TRIVIA

- Manages 419 individual units
- Cover 84 million acres
- 61 National Parks
- 84 National Monuments
- 76 National Heritage Sites
- 57 National Heritage Parks
- 30 National Memorials
- 19 National Preserves
- 18 National Recreation Areas
- 11 National Battlefields
- 10 National Seashores
- 10 National Wild Scenic Rivers and Riverways
- 9 National Military Parks
- 5 National Rivers
- 4 National Parkways
- 4 National Battlefield Parks
- 3 National Scenic Trails
- 3 National Lakeshores
- 2 National Reserves
- 1 National Battlefield Sites
- 1 International Historic Site
- 11 other designations (e.g. National Mall)

Appetizers & Beverages

CAPE COD COOLER

2 ounces sloe gin
1 ounce gin
5 ounces cranberry juice
½ ounce fresh lime juice
½ ounce orgeat syrup

1. Pour the gins, cranberry juice, lime juice and orgeat syrup into a cocktail shaker half-filled with ice cubes. Shake well.
2. Strain into a Collins glass ¾ filled with ice cubes. Garnish with a slice of lime and serve.

Serves 2

Cook's Note: Orgeat syrup is a sweet syrup made from almonds, sugar, and rose water or orange flower water.

STRAWBERRY SPARKLER

½ cup lemon juice
1 cup orange juice
½ cup superfine sugar
1 pint strawberries, washed, hulled and quartered
1 750 ml bottle Rosé wine
1 750 ml bottle Champagne, chilled
2 (7-ounce) bottles carbonated water, chilled

1. Place lemon juice, orange juice and sugar in pitcher and stir to dissolve sugar.
2. Add strawberries and Rosé wine and refrigerate several hours.
3. Just before serving, add Champagne and carbonated water.

Makes 3 quarts

MINT JULEP

2 cups granulated sugar
2 cups water
sprigs of fresh mint
crushed ice
Kentucky Bourbon Whisky
silver julep cups

1. Make a simple syrup by boiling sugar and water together for five minutes. Cool and place in a covered container with six or eight sprigs of fresh mint, then refrigerate overnight.
2. Make one julep at a time by filling a julep cup with crushed ice, adding one tablespoon mint syrup and two ounces of Kentucky Whisky. Stir rapidly with a spoon to frost the outside of the cup. Garnish with a sprig of fresh mint.

Cook's Note: Not a lot of homes have silver julep cups so instead use a nice double old-fashion glass.

From the opening of the first national park in 1905 through 2018, 14,326,829,519 individuals visited the parks. This number does not reflect visitors to parks that do not count visitors.

THE RAID ON HARPERS FERRY

Harpers Ferry is a small beautiful town located in West Virginia where the Potomac and Shenandoah Rivers converge. Yet in October 1859, the town became the last stand of abolitionist John Brown. Brown believed he could free the slaves and that war would accomplish his goals. His raid on the Federal armory, arsenal and rifle factory was also a turning point in American history, away from compromise and towards war. Determined to seize the 100,000 weapons at the Arsenal and to use the Blue Ridge Mountains for guerrilla warfare, abolitionist Brown launched his raid on Sunday evening, October 16, 1859. His 21-man "army of liberation" seized the Armory and several other strategic points. Thirty-six hours after the raid began, with most of his men killed or wounded, Brown was captured in the Armory fire enginehouse (now known as "John Brown's Fort") when U.S. Marines stormed the building. Brown was eventually found guilty of treason and was hanged on December 2, 1859.

AMERICA BEGINS HERE

www.nps.gov/casa

Castillo de San Marco, is located in St. Augustine, FL which is considered to be the oldest city in America. Throughout its history, six flags have flown over the Fort. Beginning with the Spanish, then British (1763), back to the Spanish (1764), then to United States (1821), over to Confederate States of America (1861), and then back to the United States in 1862. The Fort is the only surviving 17th century military construction in the country and the oldest masonry fortress in the United States. It is a prime example of the "bastion system" of fortification, the culmination of hundreds of years of military defense engineering. It is also unique for the material used in its construction. The Castillo is one of only two fortifications in the world built out of a semi-rare form of limestone called coquina (The other is Fort Matanzas National Monument 14 miles south).

SUNSET SANGRIA

1½ liters dry red wine
3 cups orange juice, freshly squeezed
1 quart club soda
juice of 4 limes
juice of 3 lemons
½ cup granulated sugar
½ cup brandy
1 lemon, sliced for garnish
1 orange, sliced for garnish

1. Mix all ingredients, except garnishes. Chill.
2. Serve over ice with lemon and orange garnish.

Makes 32 half-cup servings

Breads, Breakfasts and Brunch

Castillo de San Marco, St. Augustine

NO NIAGARA FALLS?

On March 30, 1848, residents on both sides of the border woke to silence. It took but a moment to realize that no water was thundering over Niagara Falls. For the first time, the river bed was exposed. Fish were dying. Factories and mills had to shut down because without water there was no electricity. Brave or foolish (you decide) people walked along the riverbed picking up guns, bayonets and tomahawks as souvenirs. People thought the world was coming to an end, other-thought it was for divine retribution for real or imagined misdeeds. It was finally determined that a really large chunk of lake ice had blocked the water from Lake Erie into the head of the Niagara River. No water flowed during the day on either March 30th & 31st. During that night, residents heard a low-pitched noise that got louder, all of a sudden a wall of water came roaring down the upper Niagara River. The ice dam had cleared and the river was running again.

BLUEBERRY JOHNNY CAKE

½ cup butter
1 cup sugar
2 eggs
1½ cups sifted all-purpose flour
1½ cups stone-ground yellow cornmeal
4 teaspoons baking powder
½ teaspoon fine sea salt
1¼ cups milk
2 cups fresh blueberries

1. Preheat oven to 350 degrees.
2. Cream butter and sugar. Add eggs, beat until light in color.
3. Combine flour, cornmeal, baking powder and salt.
4. Gradually add flour mixture to butter mixture alternating with milk, stirring until just mixed.
5. Fold in lightly floured blueberries.
6. Pour into buttered and floured 9 x 13-inch baking pan.
7. Bake for 40 minutes. Cool in pan on wire rack. When cool cut in squares.

Makes 16 squares

BLUEBERRY LEMON BREAD

1½ cups unbleached all-purpose flour
1 teaspoon baking powder
¼ teaspoon fine sea salt
6 tablespoons butter
1½ cups granulated sugar
2 eggs
2 tablespoons lemon zest
½ cup milk
1½ cups blueberries
⅓ cup sugar
3 tablespoons fresh lemon juice

1. Preheat oven to 350 degrees. Butter and flour or spray with baking spray an 8½ x 4½ -inch loaf pan.
2. Combine flour, baking powder and salt; set aside.
3. In another bowl, cream butter and sugar until fluffy. Add eggs, beating well. Add lemon zest.
4. Add dry ingredients alternating with milk. Fold in blueberries.
5. Pour into loaf pan and bake until golden brown, approximately 1¼ hours.
6. For glaze, mix together ⅓ cup sugar and lemon juice in saucepan and bring to a boil. Poke holes in bread with toothpick and pour the glaze over the bread. Cool 30 minutes.

Makes 1 loaf

RELIGIOUS FREEDOM and ROGER WILLIAMS

Roger Williams did not believe that the Colonists were true believers in religious freedom, so he moved to what is now Rhode Island. He established a community where he said all religions could practice their beliefs without persecution. The first Jewish settlers arrived in New Amsterdam in 1654, but the true test of religious tolerance occurred when a ship pulled into what is now Newport Harbor carrying fifteen families of Sephardic Jews from Barbados. In 1677, the members of the Congregation Jeshuat Israel purchased and consecrated property as a Jewish cemetery. Through the years more members arrived, and in 1763 the first synagogue was dedicated and named the Touro Synagogue after their first spiritual leader, Isaac Touro. In 1790 George Washington came to Newport and in a letter "To the Hebrew Congregation in Newport," declared that the new nation would "… give to bigotry no sanction, to persecution no assistance." These few words affirmed the founding fathers' commitment to the principals of religious freedom as a cornerstone of democracy in America.

THE GUN THAT WON THE WEST

The famous colt six shooter was manufactured in Hartford, Connecticut. The first practical "revolving pistol" was invented by Samuel Colt and first manufactured in 1836. Colonel Samuel Colt and his Colt Armory launched the second industrial revolution by combining interchangeable parts, precision machining, and the assembly line to create "The American System of Manufacturing." The Colt revolver changed the military by giving the user the capacity to shoot six bullets without reloading. Samuel Colt founded Colt Patent Firearm Manufacturing Company and ran it until his death at age of 47 when his wife took over and ran it successfully for the next 39 years. As you drive through Hartford, you can see the blue dome with stars and a colt rampart on top of it.

DATE NUT BREAD

1 (8-ounce) package dates, pitted
1 teaspoon baking soda
¾ cup boiling water
1½ cups unbleached all-purpose flour
1 cup granulated sugar
½ teaspoon fine sea salt
1 egg
1 teaspoon pure vanilla extract
1 tablespoon butter, melted
½ cup walnuts, chopped

1. Preheat oven to 350 degrees. Spray a loaf pan with non-stick baking spray.
2. Cut dates in half lengthwise. Add baking soda to water and bring to a boil and pour over dates. Let stand until you mix the dry ingredients.
3. Mix dry ingredients; add date mixture, egg, vanilla, butter, and nuts.
4. Bake for 40-60 until a tester comes out clean.

Makes 1 delicious loaf

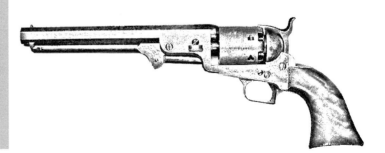

MALBONE HOUSE VIRGINIA SPOON BREAD

www.malbone.com

1 cup white cornmeal
1 cup boiling water
1 tablespoon butter, very soft
½ teaspoon fine sea salt
1 egg, well beaten
1½ teaspoons baking powder
½ cup milk
butter

1. Preheat oven to 375 degrees.
2. Sift cornmeal into mixing bowl, pour boiling water over it; blend.
3. Add butter and stir until butter melts. Add salt and egg; blend well. Stir in baking powder and milk.
4. Pour into a well-buttered deep baking dish and bake 40–45 minutes. Serve hot with butter.

Serves 8

Newport Cooks

OLD IRONSIDES

Ay, tear her tattered ensign down!
Long has it waved on high,
And many an eye has danced to see
That banner in the sky...

In 1830, it was erroneously reported that the U.S. Navy was going to scrap the vessel Old Ironsides. This led Oliver Wendell Holmes to write the above poem. Old Ironsides is the nickname for the USS Constitution, the oldest commissioned warship afloat in the world. The poem, along with public outcry, saved the famous frigate from demise. Old Ironsides got her name because bullets could not penetrate her seven-inch tough oak sides. Built from 1794-1797 at Edmund Hartt's shipyard in Boston, the ship last saw battle in the War of 1812; never in her long career did she lose a battle. In 1998, a celebration of naval vessels and tall ships from around the world descended on Boston Harbor to honor the USS Constitution and participate in its 200th birthday party. She is currently in berth at the Charlestown Naval Yard.

PLANTAIN BREAD

1 cup ripe plantain, mashed
2 cups flour, less 2 tablespoons
½ teaspoon baking soda
2 teaspoons baking powder

1. Preheat oven to 325 degrees. Grease and flour loaf pan.
2. Combine the flour, baking soda, baking powder and salt.
3. Mash plantain. Beat the eggs and blend in the oil, sugar, rind and plantain.
4. Add the flour mixture and blend well.
5. Pour into loaf pan and bake for 30 minutes.

Makes 1 loaf or 12 muffins

The Rampant Colt is the symbol of Colt Firearms. The "Rampant Colt" is an ancient symbol of a Stallion carrying a broken spear continuing the battle after his rider has fallen. The Colt and Dome have been replaced over the years. Coltsville was authorized under the Defense Spending bill in December 2014. It is waiting a for property transfer to be completed and it will then be a part of the National Parks.

BANANA MUFFINS

I've tried many banana recipes, and this is just about my favorite one. Enjoy!

1 teaspoon of baking powder
1 teaspoon of baking soda
½ teaspoon fine sea salt
1½ cups of all-purpose unbleached flour
3 large bananas, as ripe as possible
¼ cup of sugar
1 egg, lightly beaten
½ cup of melted unsalted butter

1. Preheat oven to 375 degrees.
2. Coat muffin pan with non-stick baking spray.
3. In a medium bowl combine the baking powder, baking soda, salt and flour.
4. In a large bowl mash the bananas; add the sugar and egg. Then add the melted butter.
5. Mix in the dry ingredients.
6. Spoon into muffin pan.
7. Bake for 17-20 minutes, until toothpick comes out clean.

Makes 12 muffins

APPLE SCONES WITH MAPLE CREAM SAUCE

2 cups all-purpose flour
4 teaspoons baking powder
¾ teaspoon fine sea salt
⅓ cup granulated sugar
6 tablespoons cold butter
¾ cup cream
1 egg
1 teaspoon vanilla
1 cup finely chopped tart apple
1 tablespoon butter
½ teaspoon cinnamon
pinch of nutmeg
1 cup pure New York maple syrup
½ cup heavy cream

1. Preheat oven to 375 degrees.
2. In a large mixing bowl, stir together flour, baking powder, salt and sugar. Cut in butter as if making a pie crust.
3. In a separate bowl, beat egg and cream together. Stir into dry mix, along with chopped apple.
4. Turn mixture out onto floured surface and knead until liquid is evenly absorbed.
5. Pat dough about an inch thick and cut into triangles. Bake about 15 minutes or until golden brown.
6. To make maple cream, melt butter in a small saucepan; add cinnamon and nutmeg. Add syrup and bring to gentle boil. Slowly whisk in cream and whisk constantly until the syrup is reduced by about a third. Serve over hot split scones. Also delicious on pancakes or waffles.

Makes 8 scones

BEJEWELED COLORS OF FALL

One of the nation's youngest national parks, the Marsh-Billings-Rockefeller is focused on conservation history and the evolving nature of land stewardship in America. Established by Congress in 1992, the park seeks to put the idea of conservation stewardship into a modern context, interpreting the idea of place and the ways in which humans can balance natural resource conservation with the requirements of our twenty-first century world. It also incorporates the Billings Farm & Museum which is a working dairy farm and museum of agricultural and rural life. The best time to visit the park is in late September, early October when the colors of autumn are vividly displayed.

CRANBERRY APRICOT ALMOND SCONES

1 cup dried apricots, diced
1 cup dried cranberries
orange juice
1 cup sour cream
1 teaspoon baking soda
4 cups unbleached all-purpose flour
1 cup granulated sugar
2 teaspoons baking powder
¼ teaspoon cream of tartar
1 teaspoon fine sea salt
1 cup cold butter
1 large egg
2 teaspoons almond extract
2 cups confectioners' sugar
½ teaspoon almond extract
half & half

1. Soak dried cranberries and apricots in orange juice overnight. Make sure fruit is covered.
2. In a small bowl, blend the sour cream and baking soda, and set aside.
3. Preheat oven to 350 degrees. Lightly grease a large baking sheet.
4. In large bowl, mix the flour, sugar, baking powder, cream of tartar, and salt. Cut in the butter. Stir in the sour cream mixture, egg, and almond extract into the flour mixture, until just moistened. Drain dried fruit and add to mixture. Mixture will be very dry. Knead in bowl until a soft dough forms. Divide into 3 small balls.
5. For each ball, turn dough out onto a lightly floured surface and roll or pat dough into a ¾-inch thick round. Cut into 8 wedges, and place 2 inches apart on the prepared baking sheet.
6. Bake 12 to 15 minutes, until golden brown on the bottom.
7. Prepare glaze by mixing half and half into the confectioners' sugar until the desired consistency is achieved. Add the almond extract and stir until smooth. Allow scones to cool to room temperature, drizzle glaze across the tops.

Makes 24 scones

Cook's Note: These melt-in-your-mouth scones are the perfect compliment to your coffee or tea! Enjoy!

JORDAN POND HOUSE POPOVERS

jordanpondhouse.com

2 large eggs
1 cup whole milk
1 cup unbleached all-purpose flour
¼ teaspoon fine sea salt
speck of baking soda

1. Preheat oven to 425 degrees.
2. Beat the eggs at high speed until lemon colored (2–3 minutes). On slowest speed add very slowly ½ cup of milk; beat until well mixed.
3. Sift flour, salt and soda; add slowly (with mixer on slow speed) the dry ingredients. When mixed, stop the beater, scrape the sides of the bowl with a spatula, turn to medium speed and slowly add the remaining milk; beat 2 minutes. Turn to high speed and beat 5–7 minutes. Batter should be smooth and about the thickness of heavy cream.
4. Pour the batter through a strainer, and then into well-greased muffin tins or a popover pan.
5. Bake on the middle shelf of the preheated oven for the first 15 minutes. Without opening the oven, reduce the temperature to 350 degrees and bake 15–20 minutes longer. They are best served at once, but may be kept in the warm oven for up to 5 minutes.

Makes 6 large popovers

SIEUR DE MONTS NATIONAL MONUMENT

Known to us as Acadia National Park, it was originally named after a French nobleman. In 1603, Pierre du Guast, Sieur de Monts was commissioned Lieutenant Governor of New France by King Henry IV, which gave him authority over all of North America from present-day Philadelphia to Montreal including Mt. Desert. A gentleman, George Dorr, who many say was the driving force behind preserving as much land on the island as possible, in 1901, established the Hancock County Trustees of Public Reservations. By 1913, the corporation had amassed over 6,000 acres and decided to turn it over to the federal government. In 1916 it became Sieur de Monts National Monument and the man who created it became its first superintendent. In 1929 the park changed to Acadia, and today the park protects over 47,000 acres. As Americans we should all be thankful for these individuals who preserved the "oceans, forests, lakes, and mountains" of our country for all to enjoy.

Encyclopedia Britannia, 1911 Edition

Breads, Breakfast, & Brunch

MYSTIC SEAPORT ENGLISH MUFFINS

6 cups sifted flour, divided
⅓ cup non-fat dry milk powder
1½ tablespoons sugar
1 teaspoon fine sea salt
2 packages active dry yeast
2½ cups warm water (110°)
½ cup (1 stick) butter, melted
shortening and/or vegetable oil
cornmeal
4-inch muffin rings.

1. Sift together 3 cups flour, powdered milk, sugar, salt and yeast into large mixing bowl. Stir in warm water and mix well. Cover bowl and let rise in a warm, draft-free place for 1½ hours until doubled in bulk.
2. Grease baking sheets with shortening and sprinkle with cornmeal. Lightly coat insides of muffin rings with shortening or baking spray.
3. Slowly stir melted butter and remaining 3 cups flour into dough until all is well blended. Dough will be sticky.
4. Coat hands with vegetable oil. Pinch off about 3 ounces of dough (slightly smaller than a tennis ball) and place in center of muffin ring on prepared baking sheet; attach dough to sides of ring by gently pushing with fingers. Sprinkle lightly with cornmeal. Proceed until all dough is used.
5. Cover baking sheets with plastic wrap and let rise in warm, draft-free place until muffins are doubled in size.
6. Preheat oven to 350 degrees. Gently remove plastic wrap and bake muffins about 15 minutes or until light brown.
7. Remove from baking sheet to wire rack with spatula. When cool, remove muffin rings. Muffins freeze well.

Makes about 15 muffins

UNDER THE SEA

In July, 1951, the U.S. Congress authorized construction of the world's first nuclear submarine. President Harry S. Truman laid her keel in Groton, Connecticut in June, 1952, and First Lady Mamie Eisenhower christened the sub as it slid into the Thames River in 1954. The sub took its first voyage a year later under the command of Commander Wilkinson who said, "Underway On Nuclear Power." In 1958 it conducted "Operation Sunshine" and made the first crossing of the North Pole by a ship. After a career spanning 25 years and over a half a million miles covering the globe, the first nuclear ship was decommissioned. USS Nautilus was designated a National Historic Landmark and in 1986 she was brought home to Groton where thousands tour her annually.

PANNUKAKKU
www.foodiewithfamily.com

A Pannukakku is a high-rising Finnish pancake. Described as a "breakfast custard," but similar to a popover or Yorkshire Pudding in texture. This dish is popular in Northern Michigan and is featured at Suomi's Home Bakery.

4 tablespoons butter, cut into three or four pieces
4 large eggs
1 cup unbleached all-purpose flour
1 cup milk preferably whole milk but 2% is alright
1 pinch of fine sea salt
¼ teaspoon pure vanilla extract

1. Preheat oven to 400 degrees. Place an 8- or 9-inch square pan in the oven with the butter in it. The butter should melt, but not brown.
2. Place the eggs, flour, milk, salt, and vanilla in a blender. Blend on high, scraping the sides, if necessary, until the mixture is smooth.
3. When the butter is fully melted, pull the oven rack out and pour the batter into the hot pan. Push the rack carefully back into the oven and bake for 30-40 minutes, or until pancake has puffed quite high and is a deep golden brown. Use a tester to make sure pancake is done.
4. Remove the pan from the oven, cut immediately into square and serve with your choice of topping.

Cook's Note: Can place many different items on top including sauté apples and cinnamon or caramel sauce or maple syrup with brown sugar. The pancake would also be delicious with blueberry or raspberry sauce poured on top. Be decadent! Serve with ice cream.

COPPER COUNTRY
www.nps.gov/kewe

Copper Country is in the Upper Peninsula of Michigan and the home of Keweenaw National Historic Park. The history of the region goes back over 7,000 years. Native Americans began mining from small pits in the region as far back as 3,000 B.C. Mining continued in the area until 1995 and in its heyday it was the world's greatest producer of copper. The peak production years were during World War I when 125,000 tons were mined. The Park was established in 1992 and is partially privatized and is made up of two primary units, the Calumet and Quincy Units and 21 cooperating "Heritage Sites" located on federal, state, and privately owned land in and around the Keweenaw Peninsula. The National Park Service owns about 1,700 acres in the two units.

APPLE MUFFIN

The official muffin of New York State, the Apple Muffin, was created by elementary school children in North Syracuse, New York.

½ cup walnuts, chopped
½ cup brown sugar
¼ cup unbleached all-purpose flour
1 teaspoon cinnamon
1 teaspoon lemon peel
2 tablespoons melted butter
2 cups unbleached all-purpose flour
¾ cup brown sugar
½ cup granulated sugar
2 teaspoons baking soda
½ teaspoon fine sea salt
1½ teaspoon cinnamon
½ teaspoon cloves
½ teaspoon nutmeg
3 eggs, slightly beaten
2 cups apples, coarsely chopped
½ cup dried cranberries
½ cup walnuts
½ cup butter, melted
4 ounces cream cheese, cut into small pieces
½ teaspoon vanilla

1. Preheat oven to 375 degrees. Spray muffin tins with non-stick baking spray.
2. Topping: combine first six ingredients; set aside.
3. Combine flour, brown sugar, baking soda, salt, and spices. Set aside.
4. Beat eggs; add apples, dried cranberries, walnuts, eggs, butter, cream cheese, and vanilla; mix well.
5. Add dry ingredients, a little at a time, to the apple mixture. Stir until just combined. Do not over-mix.
6. Fill muffin tins ¾ full; sprinkle with topping.
7. Bake for 20-25 minutes or until tester comes out clean.

Makes 24 muffins

KISSING POST

The Kissing Post is a column outside the Regency Room on Ellis Island where immigrants were reunited with waiting friends and relatives who had preceded them to America. The emotional and joyous scenes that took place here prompted an Ellis Island matron to write the following in 1910: "The manner in which the people of different nationalities greet each other after a separation of years is one of the interesting studies on the Island. The Italians kiss their little children but scarcely speaks to his wife, never embraces or kisses her in public. The Hungarian and Slavish [sic] people put their arms around each other and weep. The Jews of all countries kisses his wife and children as though he had all the kisses in the world, and intended to use them all up quick."

SWEET POTATO MUFFINS

1¼ cups granulated sugar
1¼ cups mashed sweet potato (fresh or canned)
½ cup butter, at room temperature
2 large eggs, at room temperature
1½ cups unbleached all-purpose flour
2 teaspoons baking powder
1 teaspoon cinnamon
¼ teaspoon nutmeg
¼ teaspoon fine sea salt
1 cup milk
½ cup dried cranberries, chopped
¼ cup pecans, chopped
2 tablespoons granulated sugar
¼ teaspoon cinnamon

1. Preheat oven to 400 degrees. Grease two 12-cup muffin tin or fill with paper liners.
2. Beat the sugar, sweet potatoes, and butter together until smooth; add eggs and blend.
3. Sift together flour, baking powder, spices and salt. Add alternately with the milk to the sweet potato mixture, stirring just to blend.
4. Fold in cranberries and nuts. Fill muffin cups ¾ full.
5. Mix sugar and cinnamon and sprinkle on top. Bake 25-30 minutes.

Makes 24 muffins

Breads, Breakfast, & Brunch

MANY ASPECTS OF MISSISSIPPI DELTA
www.nps.gov/mide

This region of the Mississippi brought us "The Blues, Eudora Welty, Richard Wright, Tennessee Williams, Tammy Wynette, James Grisham, Civil War and Civil Rights, The Great Flood, Bogues and Bayous, Plantations, The Great Migration, Rock 'n' Roll, Soul Food, King Cotton, The River, Precision Agriculture, Catfish, Gospel, Immigrants' Stories, Highway 61, Segregation, Integration, Share Cropping, Freedom Songs, Freedom Summer, Folk Tales, Swamp Forests, Hunting Clubs, hot tamale and who can forget Oprah." Elvis came from the delta as did many more great artists. The Mississippi Delta is not part of the delta of the Mississippi River. It is actually part of an alluvial plain which is created by regular flooding of the land over thousands of years of the Mississippi and Yazoo Rivers. The region covers 7,000 sq. miles and is some of the most fertile land in the world. Cotton was King in the region and sweet potatoes from the area are top-notch to this day.

OHIO'S NATIONAL PARK

www.nps.gov/cuva

While Yosemite has the Half-Dome; Yellowstone has "Old Faithful;" Arcadia has spectacular vistas; Cuyahonga Valley National Park has scenic open spaces. Humans have occupied the valley for over 12,000 years. Throughout the centuries humans have had both a positive and negative impact on the valley. The story behind the formation of the National Park highlights the effect local citizens and political leaders can have when they work together. It is a desire by locals too not only saving landmarks, but restoring the landscape to be less polluted, better environment for wildlife and a model for sustainable living. After much ado, President Gerald Ford signed the legislation on December 27, 1974, establishing Cuyahoga Valley National Recreation Area (CVNRA), but it was in name only. Over the next 34 years, Congress authorized over $200 million to purchase land and restore nearly 100 historic structures. Today more than 2,000 volunteers donate over 74,000 hours to realize the park's mission.

BRAN CRANBERRIES MUFFINS

1 cup orange juice
1 cup dried cranberries
2 cups All Bran® Buds
1½ cups 2% milk
1¼ cups all-purpose flour
½ cup sugar
4 teaspoons baking powder
¼ teaspoon fine sea salt
2 eggs
¾ cup vegetable oil
zest of 1 orange

1. Soak dried cranberries overnight in orange juice.
2. Soak bran cereal in milk overnight to soften.
3. Preheat oven to 400 degrees. Spray muffin tins with baking spray.
4. Sift together flour, sugar, baking powder and salt; set aside.
5. In large bowl, combine softened bran mixture, egg and oil; mix well. Add flour mixture, stirring only until combined. Drain cranberries and add to mixture along with the orange zest and stir lightly. To obtain a very light, tender muffin, stir as little as possible but still combine ingredients. Fill muffin tins ¾ full.
6. Place in oven and bake at 400 degrees for 10 minutes. Reduce heat to 350 degrees and bake another 35 minutes. Serve warm.

Makes 12 muffins

DIRT BOMBS

www.cottagestreetbakery.com

3 cups unbleached all-purpose flour
1 tablespoon baking powder
½ teaspoon fine sea salt
½ teaspoon ground nutmeg
¼ teaspoon cardamom
¾ cup unsalted butter
1 cup granulated sugar
2 large eggs
1 cup whole milk
¾ cup unsalted butter, melted
½ cup granulated sugar
1½ teaspoons ground cinnamon

1. Preheat oven to 400 degrees with the rack in the center position.
2. Generously coat a 12 cup standard muffin tin with butter.
3. Sift the flour, baking powder, salt, nutmeg, and cardamom into a mixing bowl. In a separate bowl, either by hand or using an electric mixer cream the butter and sugar until light and fluffy.
4. Mix in the eggs; add the dry ingredients alternating with the milk in two additions, mixing gently by hand to incorporate all the ingredients. Scrape down the sides and bottom of the bowl to be sure to incorporate all the flour. The batter will be on the stiff side, but airy. Do not overmix or beat the batter as this will make the muffins tough.
5. Scrape and spoon the batter into the muffin tin without smoothing the top.
6. Bake for about 25 minutes or until tops are golden brown and a tester put in the center comes out clean and dry.
7. Turn out on rack as soon as muffins are cool enough to touch.
8. Add the melted butter in a shallow bowl and mix the sugar and cinnamon together in a separate bowl. Dip the muffin (all of it) in butter. Use a pastry brush to cover areas not touched by dipping. Immediately roll the muffins in the cinnamon sugar mixture. Serve warm or at room temperature.

Yields: 12 Dirt Bombs

Acadia is the oldest park east of the Mississippi River and the first instance where the land was donated to the federal government.

DEVONSHIRE EGGS

1 cup diced onions
1 cup diced ham or crabmeat
1 pint heavy cream
8 ounces shredded Cheddar cheese
8-10 large eggs

1. Preheat oven to 325 degrees.
2. Butter bottom and sides of a baking dish.
3. Place diced onions and ham on the bottom of the coated dish.
4. Pour cream on top.
5. Crack eggs into baking dish.
6. Top with Cheddar cheese.
7. Bake for 35-40 minutes.

Serves 8 – 10

Eaglebrook School

SAUSAGE PUFF

1 sheet frozen puff pastry, thawed
½ pound bulk sausage, cooked and drained of fat
½ cup shredded Swiss cheese (about 4 ounces)
½ cup grated Cheddar cheese (about 1 ounce)
1 large Portabella mushroom, cut into small pieces
⅛ teaspoon freshly ground black pepper
¼ teaspoon parsley
1 tablespoon melted butter

1. Preheat oven to 425 degrees. Spray a baking sheet with non-stick baking spray.
2. Mix together sausage, cheeses, mushroom, and black pepper; set aside.
3. Unfold puff pastry onto a lightly floured 20-inch long sheet of waxed paper. Roll into a 9 x 15-inch rectangle, using a floured rolling pin. Spread filling down center of pastry sheet. Fold pastry over filling, folding short sides in first, then fold over the two large sides, envelope style. Pinch seams closed. Place seam side down onto prepared baking sheet. Remove waxed paper. Brush with melted butter.
4. Bake 10 minutes; reduce oven temperature to 375 degrees. Bake until golden brown, about 30 minutes more. Transfer baking sheet to wire rack to cool slightly. Cut into slices.

Serves 4 to 6

GRAN MARINER FRENCH TOAST

½ cup (1 stick) unsalted butter
1 cup packed brown sugar
1 Challah bread
5 large eggs
1½ cups half-and-half
1 teaspoon pure vanilla extract
1 teaspoon Grand Marnier
¼ teaspoon fine sea salt
pure maple syrup, warmed
1 orange, sliced thin

1. Preheat oven to 350 degrees.
2. In a small heavy saucepan melt butter with brown sugar over moderate heat, stirring, until smooth and pour into a 13- x 9- by 2-inch baking dish. Cut six 1-inch thick slices from center portion of bread, reserving ends for another use. Arrange bread slices in one layer in baking dish, squeezing them slightly to fit.
3. In a bowl whisk together eggs, half-and-half, vanilla, Grand Marnier, and salt until combined well and pour evenly over bread. Chill bread mixture, covered, at least 8 hours and up to 1 day.
4. Bake, uncovered, in middle of oven until puffed and edges are pale golden, 35 to 40 minutes. Serve hot French toast immediately with pure maple syrup and garnish with sliced oranges.

Serves 2 to 4

LEMON SOUFFLÉ PANCAKES

2 cups unbleached all-purpose flour
2 tablespoons granulated sugar
1 teaspoon baking soda
½ teaspoon fine sea salt
2 large eggs, separated
1½ cups buttermilk
2 teaspoons grated lemon zest
3 tablespoons lemon juice
4 tablespoons butter, melted
pure maple syrup

1. In a large bowl, mix flour, sugar, soda and salt.
2. Separate eggs in two bowls.
3. In a small bowl, whisk together egg yolks, buttermilk, lemon peel, lemon juice, and 2 tablespoons butter.
4. In a deep bowl with a mixer on high speed, whip egg whites until they hold stiff, moist peaks.
5. Pour buttermilk mixture into flour mixture; stir to blend. Add egg whites and fold gently to blend.
6. On a buttered griddle or 10 to 12-inch frying pan over medium heat, pour batter in ½- cup portions, without portions touching.
7. Cook, until golden brown on each side, turning once, 4 to 5 minutes total. Keep warm. Repeat to cook remaining pancakes.
8. Serve warm with maple syrup.

Makes 8 pancakes

FIGHTING FOR PRINCIPLE AND FREEDOM

www.nps.gov/cane

Kentucky was one of the few slave states that did not join the Confederacy. When Abraham Lincoln signed the Emancipation Proclamation it did not include Kentucky. Elijah Marrs was one of about 10,000 African-Americans who eventually came to Camp Nelson. It was a Union Army depot during the Civil War that became a recruiting center for black soldiers and a refugee camp for their families. In his autobiography, Marrs wrote that, "If we staid at home we would have been murdered. If we join the army and were slain in battle, we would at least die fighting for principle and freedom." Camp Nelson represents the courage and determination of formerly enslaved African Americans to secure their own emancipation. It also illustrates the nation's struggle to define the meaning of freedom during and after the Civil War.

APPLE FRITTATA

1 tablespoon vegetable oil
1 medium onion, chopped
1 green bell pepper, chopped
1 clove garlic, crushed
1 medium apple, peeled, cored, and sliced
4 eggs
2 tablespoons water
fine sea salt
freshly ground black pepper
⅓ cup shredded cheddar cheese

1. Heat oil in medium skillet. Add onion, bell pepper and garlic. Cook over medium-low heat, stirring occasionally, until tender.
2. Add sliced apple and cook about 4 minutes, or until tender.
3. In medium bowl, beat eggs with water, salt and pepper. Pour over apple-vegetable mixture in skillet.
4. Sprinkle with cheese. Cover skillet and cook over low heat about 10 minutes, or until eggs are set and cheese melts.

Serves 2

MONTICELLO CHEESE GRITS

3½ cups water
1 cup quick grits
4 ounces garlic cheese, shredded
1 egg, beaten
½ cup milk
4 drops Tabasco® sauce
¾ cup Cheddar cheese, grated

1. Heat water until boiling; add grits. Turn heat to low and cook grits until water is absorbed.
2. Add garlic cheese and stir until cheese is melted.
3. Combine egg, milk and Tabasco. Add to grits and mix well.
4. Pour into well-greased 1-quart casserole. Top with Cheddar cheese.
5. Bake 30 minutes.

Serves 6 to 8

NATURE'S CALLING

www.nps.gov/shen/index.htm

The Shenandoah National Park was named for the river running through it which flows into the Potomac River at Harpers Ferry. When we think of the Shenandoah we think beautiful vistas, waterfalls, quietness and hiking. The mountains and valley have been inhabited for thousands of years. Native Americans seasonally visited this area to hunt, gather food, source materials for stone tools, and trade. The Europeans arrived in the 1700s, first as hunters and trappers and then farmers, miners and loggers. By the late 1800s an increasingly urban American society yearned for places of recreation and refuge. There were no national parks in the eastern part of the country and a call arose for a Park accessible to large population centers. It wasn't until 1935 that the Park was established.

KUCHEN
The Official State Dessert of South Dakota

1 package dry yeast
1 tablespoon granulated sugar
¼ cup lukewarm water
2 cups warm whole or 2% milk
½ cup granulated sugar
1 teaspoon fine sea salt
2 beaten eggs
¼ cup vegetable oil
4-5 cups flour

1. In a large bowl, dissolve the yeast and sugar into the warm water. In a stainless steel pan, scald the milk by bringing to a boil and then reducing heat. The milk should have a film on top of it.
2. Add sugar, salt, eggs and vegetable oil into the milk. Add milk mixture into the bowl of yeast and water and mix together. Mix in 4 to 5 cups of flour; mix well. Knead until dough is smooth and elastic, sprinkle with a little flour at a time. Let rise one hour. Put in warm place to rise until double in bulk.
3. Divide the dough into eight equal pieces. Roll each to about ¼-inch thick and place in a greased pie pan so that the dough covers the bottom and comes about halfway up the side. Let dough rise in the pan for 15 minutes. Add a layer of thinly sliced apples, peaches, prunes, strawberries or other fruit if desired.

Filling:
2 cups sweet cream or sour cream
2 eggs beaten
½ cup granulated sugar
2 tablespoons all-purpose flour
½ teaspoon pure vanilla extract
cinnamon

1. Preheat oven to 350 degrees.
2. Top the fruit with cream filling. Sprinkle with cinnamon.
3. Bake for 25 to 30 minutes or until brown.

Topping:
2 cups granulated sugar
2 cups all-purpose flour
1 cup butter

1. Mix the sugar, flour and butter together so that it is somewhere between smooth and lumpy. Pour the topping on and bake it in the oven for about 30 minutes at 350 degrees. After the kuchen comes out of the oven, let it set for five minutes, then remove from the pan and let it cool.

Source: Adapted from South Dakota Magazine

CHEESE BLINTZES WITH CINNAMON HOT APPLE SAUCE

3 large eggs
1 cup milk
2 tablespoons vegetable oil
½ teaspoon fine sea salt
¾ cup unbleached all-purpose flour
2 tablespoons unsalted butter, melted
2 cups cottage cheese
1 lightly beaten egg
2 tablespoons granulated sugar
1 tablespoon unsalted butter, melted
1 teaspoon pure vanilla extract
¾ teaspoon fine sea salt
cinnamon hot apple sauce (page 118)

1. Place eggs, milk, oil and salt in medium bowl; blend well. Add the flour and blend until just combined.
2. Place butter in an 8-inch fry pan, tilting the pan so the butter flows to coat the bottom.
3. Add just enough batter to make a very thin pancake. Cook until the edges begin to turn golden. Shake the pan to loosen the pancakes. Quickly turn the pancake out onto a paper towel, browned side up. Repeat with the remaining butter and batter, stacking the cooked pancakes between sheets of paper towels.
4. Arrange a pancake, browned side up, and place a heaping spoonful of Cinnamon Hot Apple Sauce filling just above the center. Fold the sides toward the middle, overlapping the edges. Fold down the top to seal in the filling; then roll the pancake. You want to make a neat little packet.
5. Arrange the blintzes, seam side down, on a heated griddle or in a large skillet brushed with butter. Cook until browned, turning once.

Makes 14-18 blintzes

FROM COLONIES TO STATES
www.nps.gov/frst

In the spring of 1776, the Continental Congress realized that reconciliation with Great Britain was not going to happen. All of the English governors of the 13 colonies had either fled back to Britain or had been imprisoned. The Congress advised the colonies to govern themselves. All but two of the colonies had new constitutions; Connecticut and Rhode Island used their old charters. With these actions, they moved from colonies into sovereign independent states. On December 7, 1787, Delaware became the first state of the fledging nation.

Breads, Breakfast, & Brunch

NIAGARA FALLS TRIVIA

- It is the most visited waterfall in the world.
- The formation of the Falls began at the end of the Ice Age.
- There are really three waterfalls, Horseshoe, Bridal Veil, and American Falls
- The first person to see and describe the Falls at length was Father Louis Hennepin, a French priest who accompanied LaSalle on his expedition to the Niagara region in 1678.
- The more spectacular Horseshoe Fall is 98 percent Canadian, while Bridal Veil and American Falls are on the American side of the border.
- The Falls are 170 feet tall and 3,660 feet wide
- Approximately 65,000 cubic feet per second is the average volume of water going over the Falls. A large portion of the water is diverted for hydro-electric power before it reaches the Falls.
- In 1804, Napoleon Bonaparte's young brother, Jerome, honeymooned with his American bride at the Falls.
- The Niagara River is actually a strait, connecting two large bodies of water, Lake Erie and Lake Ontario.
- Niagara Falls State Park is the oldest state park in the United States.

CRUSTLESS ASPARAGUS QUICHE

2 cups sliced asparagus
6 egg whites
2 whole eggs
⅓ cup diced onion
½ cup (low-fat) feta cheese, optional parmesan cheese
½ cup diced tomatoes
¼ teaspoon freshly ground black pepper
fine sea salt to taste

1. Preheat oven to 350 degrees.
2. Combine all ingredients in a medium mixing bowl and pour into a quiche pan or 9-inch glass pie plate.
3. Bake for approximately 45 minutes or until filling is set.

Serves 6 - 8

Soups and Salads

NIAGARA FALLS

TURNING POINT OF THE REVOLUTIONARY WAR

www.nps.gov/kimo

On October 7, 1780, a 1,000 militiamen helped change the direction of the War in the South. The battle took place on King's Mountain in South Carolina. The battle was between untrained American Whigs (Patriots) and American Tories (Loyalist or Royalist). It only took one hour for the Patriots under the command of Colonel William Campbell to decimate the Tories. One reason is that the Patriots were far superior marksmen. Nearly all the Tories including their leader English Colonel Patrick Ferguson were killed. One of the forces behind the Patriots push was a message received a month earlier that if the "officers of the western waters" did not "desist from their opposition to the British army and take protection under his standard, he would march his army over the mountains, hang their leaders, and lay their country waste with fire and sword." This was like waving a red flag in front of a bull.

SHE CRAB SOUP

2 tablespoons unsalted butter
1 small onion, grated
3 celery stalks, minced
1 tablespoon all-purpose flour
fine sea salt to taste
freshly ground white pepper to taste
¼ teaspoon ground mace
½ teaspoon dried thyme
½ teaspoon Worcestershire® sauce
½ teaspoon Tabasco® sauce
splash of fresh lemon juice
2 cups heavy cream
2 cups milk
1 pound crabmeat
½ cup dry sherry wine
paprika
1 tablespoon finely-chopped fresh parsley

1. Make roux by melting the butter in a large skillet over medium heat and sauté the onion and celery until soft. Sprinkle the flour over the vegetables, stir, and cook 5 minutes.
2. Add salt, pepper, mace, thyme, Worcestershire® sauce, Tabasco®, and a splash of lemon juice; Simmer briefly.

3. Add the cream and milk; heat almost to scalding, stirring constantly.
4. Add the crabmeat and stir.
5. Heat just long enough to warm through.
6. Add the sherry wine and serve at once, garnished with paprika and chopped parsley.

Serves 8

Cook's Note: Different areas have different crabmeat. States on the east coast use Chesapeake Bay Blue Crab. Dungeness Crab is sweet, tender and flaky and come from Alaska and the west coast. Jumbo lump crabmeat comes from larger crabs and is the meat from the two large muscles connected to the swimming legs.

> "There is nothing so American as our national parks....The fundamental idea behind the parks... is that the country belongs to the people, that it is in process of making for the enrichment of the lives of all of us."
> President Franklin D. Roosevelt

MONUMENTS TO THE FALLEN
www.nps.gov/nama

Many a time, I have stood on the steps of either the Lincoln Memorial or the Capitol and looked down the Mall and felt a sense of peace at the view. It is awe inspiring to see the reflecting pool and the amazing building on each side of it. It is 1.9 miles between the two buildings. The Washington Monument sits at 1.2 miles from the Capitol. Today the Mall is the home to several monuments to honor the Fallen. There are monuments to remember the Korean War, Vietnam, and the WWII Memorial and the tens of thousands of men who lost their lives. To visit these memorials is highly emotional especially if you know names that are on the Wall. Several other monuments are in memory of Martin Luther King, Thomas Jefferson, Ulysses S. Grant and Franklin Delano Roosevelt. The Mall is also host to the Independence Day Celebration and the National Christmas Tree Celebration. It has also been known to host many a rally and march.

HADDOCK CHOWDER

¼ cup salt pork, chopped finely
1 large onion, coarsely chopped
1½ tablespoons all-purpose flour
1 (8-ounce) bottle clam juice
1½ cups milk
½ teaspoon freshly ground black pepper
¼ teaspoon fine sea salt
1 large potato, peeled and chopped
12 ounces haddock, skinned, boned and cut into 1½-inch chunks

1. In a large saucepan, cook salt pork on high heat for 2 minutes; stirring occasionally. Add onion and continue to cook until onion has softened.
2. Blend in flour; gradually pour in clam juice and whisk until combined. Add milk, pepper, salt and potato; bring to a simmer.
3. Reduce heat to low and simmer uncovered until potatoes are tender and chowder has thickened. Add haddock and cook just until the fish almost flakes, about 5 minutes.

Serves 4

IRISH POTATO, LEEK AND BACON SOUP

3 pounds potatoes
1 pint heavy cream
¼ pound bacon, cooked and crumbled
1 leek, white part only, sliced, washed and diced
1 tablespoon butter
fine sea salt to taste
freshly ground black pepper to taste
chopped fresh parsley for garnish

1. Peel 2 pounds of the potatoes and cook in water to cover until soft. Pour off half the cooking water from the potatoes and reserve. Purée the cooked potatoes and the remaining water, add cream, and simmer for 5 minutes; then set aside (this is the soup base).
2. Peel and dice the remaining pound of potatoes. Cover with water and boil until cooked but still firm. Drain and hold.
3. Melt butter in sauté pan and sauté leeks until soft. Add cooked diced potatoes, bacon and leeks to the soup base. Season to taste with salt and pepper. If too thick, thin with reserved potato cooking water or additional cream. Serve hot, garnished with parsley.

Serves 6

CORN AND CRAB BISQUE

¼ cup plus 3 tablespoons unsalted butter
6 tablespoons all-purpose flour
3 cups chopped onions fine
1 cup red bell pepper, chopped fine
1 cup celery, chopped fine
6 garlic cloves, minced
2 teaspoons dried thyme
½ cup dry white wine
6 (8-ounce) bottles clam juice
2 cups fresh or frozen unthawed corn kernels
½ cup whipping cream
1½ tablespoons Worcestershire® sauce
½ teaspoon cayenne pepper
1 pound fresh crabmeat
3 green onions, chopped
fresh parsley, chopped
fine sea salt
freshly ground black pepper

1. Melt ¼ cup butter in small saucepan over medium-low heat. Add flour and cook 2 minutes, stirring constantly (do not brown). Remove roux from heat.
2. In a heavy large pot, melt remaining 3 tablespoons butter over medium heat. Add onions, bell pepper, and celery; sauté until onions are tender, about 10 minutes.
3. Add garlic and thyme and cook 2 minutes.
4. Add wine and simmer until wine is absorbed, about 2 minutes. Whisk in roux.
5. Add clam juice and corn and bring to boil. Simmer until soup thickens, stirring occasionally, about 15 minutes.
6. Add cream, Worcestershire sauce, and cayenne pepper and bring to simmer. Stir in crabmeat and green onions. Season to taste with salt and pepper. Sprinkle with parsley and serve.

Serves 8

On August 25, 1916, President Woodrow Wilson signed the act creating the National Park Service. The "Organic Act" states that the fundamental purpose of the NPS "is to conserve the scenery and the natural and historic objects and the wild life therein and to provide for the enjoyment of the same in such manner and by such means as will leave them unimpaired for the enjoyment of future generations."

LEGEND OF THE MAID OF THE MIST

The Maid of the Mist tour boat is named after Lelawala, the daughter of Chief Eagle Eye of the Ongiaras tribe which lived beside Niagara Falls. It seems that each year many members of the tribe were dying and no one knew why. Initially to satisfy the Gods the members of the tribe sent canoes laden with fruit, flowers and game. When that didn't work, they sent one of the beautiful maidens as a tribute. When Lelawala went over the Falls she was caught in the arms of the sons of the Thunder God, Hinum. She made an agreement with the sons that if she were told what was killing her people, she would agree to live forever behind the Falls. They told her it was a large serpent who lived in the river. She told her people how to kill the serpent that was poisoning their water. They followed her advice and the serpent, as it tried to get back to the river, got caught in the Falls, and as it was dying, its body formed a semi-circle which became Horseshoe Falls. Lelawala returned to the cave of Hinum where she reigns as the Maid of the Mist.

SENATE NAVY BEAN AND HAM SOUP

This soup is served daily in the Senate Dining Room since the early 1900s.

1 (16 ounce) package dried navy beans, soaked overnight according to package directions, drained, and rinsed
4 cups water
2 cups reduced-sodium vegetable broth
1 cup chopped yellow onion (1 small onion)
½ cup chopped peeled carrot (2 carrots)
½ cup chopped celery (3 celery stalks)
1 garlic clove, minced
1 bay leaf
½ teaspoon freshly ground black pepper
1 large, meaty roasted ham bone

1. Place beans, water, broth, onion, carrot, celery, garlic, bay leaf, and pepper in a 5 to 6-quart slow cooker; stir to combine.
2. Place ham bone in center of mixture. Cover and cook on HIGH 6 hours or LOW 8 to 10 hours until beans are tender. Remove ham bone and any gristle. Return any ham meat to soup.

Serves 6 - 8

PASTA Y FAGIOLI

6 slices bacon, cut into ½-inch pieces (or pancetta or prosciutto)
½ cup olive oil
6 cloves garlic, peeled and minced
1½ cups diced onion (about 1 medium)
4 (15½-ounce) cans white bean in liquid (Cannellini, great northern, or small white)
1 (28-ounce) can whole tomatoes, hand crushed or chopped in a blender
4 (15½-ounce) cans low-sodium, reduced-fat chicken broth
1 pound small pasta (tubettini, orzo, elbows, or orichiette), cooked al dente
fine sea salt to taste
crushed red pepper to taste
½ teaspoon dried oregano
4 tablespoons chopped fresh parsley
1 cup freshly grated Pecorino Romano cheese

1. In a large sauce pot over medium-high heat, cook the bacon until slightly crisp. Drain the fat from the bacon, but do not clean the pot.
2. In the same pot, heat the olive oil, add the garlic, and sauté until it turns golden. Add the onion, return the bacon to the pan, and sauté about 5 minutes, until the onion becomes translucent.
3. Stir in the beans with their liquid, the tomatoes, and the chicken stock, and bring to a boil, then lower the heat and simmer for 5 minutes. Add the pasta, season with sea salt and crushed red pepper. Stir in the oregano and parsley and serve immediately, passing the grated cheese on the side.

Serves 8

Cooking with the Firehouse Chef

THE PEOPLE OF HAMMERSMITH

The Saugus Iron Works, or "Hammersmith" as it was then called, was the first successful plant for the integrated production of cast and wrought iron in the new world. In 1641, the Puritans of Massachusetts Bay set in place a plan for locating iron ore and for iron making, and appointed John Winthrop Jr., son of Governor Winthrop, as its leader. He formed the Company of Undertakers of the Iron Works in New England. Winthrop set up his operation in Braintree, but it was unsuccessful and Winthrop was replaced by Richard Leader. The site on the Saugus River was chosen by Leader because of its waterpower, water transport, woodlands and raw materials. By 1646, the Saugus Works were producing iron products for Massachusetts and England. Beginning in 1650s, financial difficulties beset the iron works from which it never recovered. The last recorded blast was in 1668. Its greatest accomplishment was introducing a complex and demanding technology into the new world.

UNDERGROUND RAILROAD "CONDUCTOR"

www.nps.gov/hatu/

The Underground Railroad refers to the movement of self-emancipation of enslaved people of African descent to escape bondage and gain freedom, and the network of people and places who aided their escapes. Harriet Tubman (1820-1913) did extraordinary work with abolitionist causes and as the Underground Railroad's most famous conductor. It is said that she never ran her train off the track and she never lost a passenger. Her heroic efforts in personally leading people out of slavery to freedom in the North defined her as the "Moses of her People." Besides her work with the Underground Railroad, she served the United States Army as a spy, scout, nurse and cook and, as a result, received military recognition at her burial. The National Historical Park in Church Creek, Maryland was created by Congress in December 2014 and includes the Harriet Tubman Underground Railroad National Monument.

RIESLING ONION SOUP

1½ tablespoons butter
1½ tablespoons olive oil
1 garlic clove, minced
4 large onions
1 tablespoon all-purpose flour
2 cups Riesling wine
6 cups beef stock
fine sea salt to taste
freshly ground pepper to taste
slice of French bread
shredded Gruyere cheese

1. Melt butter with olive oil in large pot over medium heat.
2. Add minced garlic clove and 4 large onions, very thinly sliced (as whole or half rings) and cook onions until soft, about 10 to 15 minutes.
3. Sprinkle flour over softened onions and cook for about 5 minutes.
4. Pour in Riesling wine and simmer for 10 minutes.
5. Pour in chicken stock and simmer everything for about 45 minutes. Add salt and pepper to taste.
6. Ladle soup into oven-proof bowls. Place a thin slice of French bread on top of soup, sprinkle with cheese, melting it until the cheese is bubbly.

Serves 6-8

POTATO BACON SOUP

1 bay leaf
2 sprigs fresh thyme
2 sprigs fresh parsley
2 tablespoons unsalted butter
¼ cup water
2 medium onions, chopped
3 cloves garlic, chopped
6 strips good-quality bacon, cut into 1-inch pieces
2 quarts chicken stock
5 large russet baking potatoes (about 3½ pounds), peeled and coarsely chopped
1 teaspoon fine sea salt to taste
½ teaspoon freshly ground black pepper
1 cup heavy cream
2 tablespoons chopped chives
2 strips bacon, cooked and crumbled for garnish

1. Wrap the bay leaf, thyme, and parsley in a piece of cheesecloth. Tie it with butcher's string.
2. In a soup pot, combine the butter, water, onions, garlic, and bacon. Set it over medium heat. Cook, stirring occasionally, for 8 to 10 minutes or until the onions soften and the bacon fat is mostly rendered.
3. Spoon off excess fat. Add the chicken stock, potatoes, salt, pepper, and herb bundle. Turn up the heat and bring the mixture to a boil. Reduce the heat to medium and simmer, uncovered, for about 35 minutes or until the potatoes are tender. Cool slightly. Discard the herb bundle.
4. Using an immersion blender, food processor, or blender, puree the soup.
5. Before serving, stir in the cream and reheat the soup until very hot but do not boil. Taste for seasoning, add salt, if you like. Ladle the soup into bowls and sprinkle with chives or bacon.

Serves 8

OYSTER STEW

1 pint light cream
2 tablespoons butter
pinch nutmeg
1 pint (or more!) oysters and the liquor

1. Bring cream to a simmer in a double boiler.
2. Add butter and nutmeg.
3. Add oysters and liquor.
4. Serve when oysters curl and rise to the top. Oyster crackers are good floating in the bowl as well.

Serves 2

ENGLISH CHEDDAR CHOWDER

2 cups water
⅓ cup carrot, finely chopped
⅓ cup celery, finely chopped
⅓ cup scallops, finely chopped
1 medium onion, finely chopped
½ cup (1 stick) butter
½ cup all-purpose flour
4 cups milk, hot
4 cups chicken broth, hot
1 pound sharp Cheddar cheese, grated
1 tablespoon Dijon mustard
fine sea salt to taste
freshly ground black pepper to taste
cayenne pepper to taste
1 pound smoked ham, finely chopped
green scallion tops for garnish, chopped

1. In a small saucepan, bring the water to a boil and add carrot, celery, and scallions. Boil the vegetables for 5 minutes. Reserve.
2. In a soup pot, sauté the onion in the butter for 1 minute, or until soft. Blend in flour and slowly add the hot milk and hot chicken broth. Whisk the mixture constantly until it is well blended and smooth.
3. Add the cheese, the reserved vegetables and their cooking liquid, mustard, seasonings, and ham. Continue cooking the soup, whisking constantly, until cheese is melted and everything is well blended. Garnish with green scallion tops.

Serves 10

In Florida, Everglades National Park features 360 different species of birds, including the crowd-pleasing greater flamingo. And amid the old-growth bottomland hardwood forest of South Carolina's Congaree National Park, you can spy barred owls by night on the ranger-led Owl Prowl.

Soups and Salads

CHEESEBURGER CHOWDER

2 medium green peppers, chopped fine
1 onion, chopped fine
2 tablespoons all-purpose flour
½ pound ground hamburger
1 quart chicken broth
4 ounces cheddar cheese, shredded
1 pint half and half or milk

1. Sauté onions and peppers in large pot. Add hamburger and brown.
2. Add chicken broth. Mix flour with ¼ cup of broth and blend well before adding to mixture. Bring to a boil.
3. Add cheddar cheese and half & half (or milk). Stir until cheese is melted.
4. Season to taste. Serve hot with a salad and some French bread.

Serves 6 - 8

EYE OF MIAMI

Located within sight of Miami, Florida Biscayne National Park offers visitors an inside look at a parade of history covering 10,000 years. A Tequesta man free-dives for conch from a dugout canoe, a Bahamian woman watches the sunset across a tidal creek, a ship grinds against a knife-edged reef while the wind howls, and wealthy industrialists gather under a shady palm to toss horseshoes. Though the park was established for its natural history, signs are everywhere of people and the many ways they used these lands and waters. Islands reveal evidence of use by native peoples. Underwater, shipwrecks rest as silent witnesses to violent moments in time, each holding the promise of teaching us about our collective past. Biscayne National Park's Maritime Heritage Trail offers an exciting opportunity to explore the remains of some of the park's many shipwrecks. Six wrecks, spanning nearly a century and a wide variety of sizes and vessel types lay offshore. Besides the wrecks, the trail includes the Fowey Rocks Lighthouse and is known as the "Eye of Miami."

CARRIAGE ROAD OF MT. DESERT

Another lover of the natural beauty of Mt. Desert was John D. Rockefeller, Jr. He wanted to travel motor-free byways via horse and carriage. He played an integral role in the construction and placement of 45 miles of carriage roads. Rockefeller wanted the roads to be part of the landscape. He financed the construction of not only the roadways but also 16 of the 17 stone-faced bridges. Coping stones which are large blocks of granite were placed along the roads acting as guardrails. Visitors today ride over these same roads which crisscross the island. In the mid-1990s, the National Park Service undertook an extensive rehabilitation of the roadways and bridges. These roads were placed to show the island and surrounding waters to their best advantage, and I can attest that the views are sensational.

JORDAN POND LOBSTER STEW

3 tablespoons butter
1 cup fresh picked lobster meat
paprika
1 tablespoon lobster or seafood base
3 cups whole milk
1 cup light cream
freshly ground white pepper
fine sea salt
sherry

1. Melt butter over low heat, add lobster meat, paprika, and soup base (if available) and lightly sauté for about ten minutes.
2. Scald the milk and cream and add to the lobster mixture. Hold in a double boiler for serving immediately or chill under refrigeration overnight to allow the flavors to meld and gently reheat for service the next day.

Serves 4

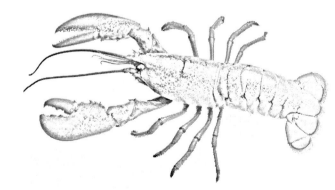

STRAWBERRY SPINACH SALAD

1 teaspoon dry mustard
1 teaspoon fine sea salt
⅓ cup granulated sugar
⅓ cup strawberry vinegar (page 117)
¾ cup canola oil
1 pound fresh spinach, washed, deveined, and torn into pieces (or baby spinach, whole)
1 pint fresh strawberries, hulled and thinly sliced
1½ tablespoons poppy seeds

1. In a medium bowl, whisk together mustard, salt, sugar, and strawberry vinegar. While vigorously whisking, pour 2 to 3 tablespoons oil into mix and whisk until well incorporated. In a thin, steady stream, whisk in remaining oil. Add spinach and strawberries; gently toss well to coat. Sprinkle poppy seeds over the top.

Serves 2 - 4

EVERGLADES TRIVIA

- Established: December 6, 1947
- Size: 1,542,526 acres. The largest subtropical wilderness in the United States features 360 different species of birds and 300 species of fish.
- The park has been designated as a UNESCO World Heritage site and International Biosphere Reserve, a Wetland of International Importance, and a specially protected area under the Cartagena Treaty.
- Take a tour of a Cold War–era Nike Missile Base. The now abandoned antiaircraft missile site was built in response to the 1962 Cuban Missile Crisis.
- Home to the elusive Florida panther. This is the only breeding population in the eastern United States.
- 36 threatened or endangered species call the Everglades home. Including the Florida Panther and the American Crocodile.
- Everglades are the only place in the world where alligators and crocodiles coexist!
- Often described as a wetland or swamp, the Everglades is really a very slow moving river better known as the "River of Grass."

GATEWAY TO FREEDOM

Before Ellis Island became known as the main entry point for immigrants entering the United States, it was a hanging site for pirates, a harbor fort, ammunition and ordinance depot named Fort Gibson, and finally into an immigration station. Prior to 1890, the individual states (rather than the Federal government) regulated immigration into the United States. On January 2, 1892, the first immigrant, Annie Moore, a 15 year old Irish girl and her two brothers were processed through Ellis Island. Over the next 62 years over 12 million came seeking a better life for themselves and their families. Despite the island's reputation as an "Island of Tears," the vast majority of immigrants were treated courteously and respectfully. In November of 1954 the last detainee, a Norwegian merchant seaman named Arne Peterssen, was released, and Ellis Island officially closed. Starting in 1984, Ellis Island underwent a major restoration, the largest historic restoration in U.S. history. The main building was reopened to the public on September 10, 1990, as the Ellis Island Immigration Museum. Today, the museum receives almost 2 million visitors annually.

WALDORF SALAD

Apple is the official fruit of New York

2 cups honey crisp apples, cored and peeled
1 cup celery, chopped
½ cup broken walnuts
¼ cup dried cranberries
¼ cup mayonnaise
½ tablespoon granulated sugar
½ teaspoon lemon juice
dash of fine sea salt
½ cup whipping cream, whipped

1. Combine apples, celery, cranberries, and nuts. Blend mayonnaise, sugar, lemon juice, and salt.
2. Fold in whipped cream and chill.

Serves 6

Soups and Salads

BROCCOLI SALAD

4 broccoli crowns
1 small red onion, finely chopped
½ pound bacon
½ cup sunflower seeds
½ cup golden raisins or dried cranberries
½ cup Monterey Jack cheese, grated
1 cup mayonnaise

1. Separate the broccoli into small florets and slice the tender part of the stems. Steam broccoli over boiling water, covered until the color brightens, about 3 minutes. Do not overcook. You want the broccoli crunchy.
2. Cook bacon and crumble. I like to cook it in the microwave. Place on a paper plate and cover with paper toweling. Cook 3 minutes, turn and cook other side 2 minutes.
3. Place broccoli, bacon, onion, seeds, raisins and cheese in bowl. Mix with mayonnaise.
4. Chill thoroughly before serving.

Serves 8

Note: Feel free to mix and change ingredients. Use pine nuts, or slivered almonds in place of sunflower seeds. I like to use dried cranberries, they add color to the dish or use a ¼ cup of each. For cheeses, try grated cheddar or a mix. Also use cauliflower in addition to broccoli or combine the two.

FOOTPATH FOR THE PEOPLE

The Appalachian Trail is a 2,180+ mile long public footpath that traverses the scenic, wooded, pastoral, wild, and culturally resonant lands of the Appalachian Mountains. It is the longest "hiking only" footpath in the world. It snakes through 14 states from Georgia to Maine. Conceived in 1921, built by private citizens, and completed in 1937, today the trail is managed by the National Park Service, US Forest Service, Appalachian Trail Conservancy, numerous state agencies and thousands of volunteers. The elevation gain/loss of hiking the entire Appalachian Trail is the equivalent of climbing Mount Everest (29,029 ft.) 16 times. About 15,000 people have hiked the entire length of the Trail since it was completed in 1937.

1800 MILES 10 DAYS

www.nps.gov/poex

Only in operation for 18 months from April 1860 until October 1861, the men of the Pony Express served an important function in getting mail from Kansas to California. Following is an ad in the Sacramento Union in March, 1860 for riders, "Men Wanted" The undersigned wishes to hire ten or a dozen men, familiar with the management of horses, as hostlers, or riders on the Overland Express Route via Salt Lake City. Wages $50 per month and found." The mail delivery was accomplished by a relay of men covering 1800 miles in 10 days. While the Pony Express was keeping the lines of communication open between the east and west, Congress was passing a bill authorizing the building of a transcontinental telegraph to connect the Missouri River and the Pacific Coast. It was on October 26, 1861 that San Francisco was in direct contact with New York City and it was on that day that the Pony Express ended.

DRIED CRANBERRY, WALNUT, AND BLUE CHEESE SALAD

3 tablespoons apple cider vinegar
1 shallot, peeled and minced
½ cup vegetable oil
coarsely ground sea salt
freshly ground black pepper
¼ cup dried cranberries
¼ cup walnut pieces
2 apples, cored and cut into ¼-inch cubes
4 ounces blue cheese, crumbled
1 pound baby spinach, rinsed and well dried

1. Combine the vinegar and shallots in a medium-sized mixing bowl. Whisk in the oil in a slow steady stream until it is completely incorporated and the mixture is slightly thickened. Season with salt and pepper to taste.
2. Add the cranberries, walnuts, and apples to the bowl with the dressing and toss to cost. Add the blue cheese and mix gently so that the cheese remains in discrete pieces. Distribute the spinach among 6 salad plates and top with the cranberry mixture.

Serves 6

PINEAPPLE PASTA PRIMAVERA

1 can pineapple chunks
3 cups cooked spiral pasta
¼ cup chopped cilantro or parsley
½ cup reduced calorie Italian salad dressing
2 cups snow peas
1 cup sliced carrots
1 cup sliced cucumbers
½ cup sliced radishes

1. Drain pineapple; reserve ¼ cup juice.
2. Combine pineapple, reserved juice, pasta and vegetables in large bowl.
3. Toss to coat.

Cook's Note: It is best to make this salad several hours or even a day ahead so that the spices and fruits can enhance the flavor.

Serves 6 - 8

PROTECTING OUR BEACHES

The first National Seashore was established in 1937, when Congress designated Cape Hatteras as the first Seashore. It wasn't until 1953 that enough land had been acquired to finally establish the park. Overall, there are 10 National Seashores. One on the Pacific Ocean, two on the Gulf coast and seven on the Eastern seaboard. Cape Cod National Seashore is the most popular with over 4 million visitors a year and 40 miles worth of beaches. The largest National Seashore encompasses the islands of two different states: Florida and Mississippi. Gulf Islands National Seashore stretches 160 miles on the Gulf of Mexico. The seven National Seashores on the east coast include Assateague Island, Canaveral, Cape Cod, Cape Hatteras, Cape Lookout, Cumberland Island, and Fire Island.

1905 SALAD

½ head iceberg lettuce
2 ripe tomatoes, cut in eighths
2 stalks celery, sliced
½ cup Swiss cheese, cut in julienne strips
½ cup ham, cut in julienne strips (or turkey or shrimp)
¼ cup green Spanish olives, pitted
2 teaspoons grated Romano cheese

1. Toss together all salad ingredients except Romano cheese.

Dressing

2 tablespoons white wine vinegar
½ cup extra-virgin Spanish olive oil
4 cloves garlic, minced
1 teaspoon Worcestershire® sauce
fine sea salt to taste
freshly ground black pepper to taste
1 teaspoon oregano
2 teaspoons lemon juice

1. Mix garlic, oregano, and Worcestershire® sauce in a bowl; beat until smooth with a wire whisk.
2. Add olive oil, gradually beating to form an emulsion. Stir in vinegar and lemon juice; season with salt and pepper.
3. Add dressing to salad and toss well. Add Romano cheese and toss one more time.

Serves 4

The Columbia Restaurant Spanish Cookbook

Cook's Note: This is a favorite of mine. The signature salad, named for the year the restaurant was founded in Tampa's Cuban district of Ybor City, was inspired by immigrants to the Cigar City.

WHAT IS AN EARTH LODGE?

The earth lodge (or mud-lodge as the Pawnees refer to it) was the dominant dwelling of Central and Northern Great Plains village Indians. These earthen structures were circular, dome-shaped dwellings with heavy timbered framework covered by layers of branches, grass, and lastly earth. These lodges were built with a technique 6000 years old. While the Earth Lodge people hunted bison and other game, they were primarily farmers. Earth lodges are well-known from the more-sedentary tribes of the Plains such as the Hidatsa, Mandan, and Arikara. The men of the village raised the frame of logs, but the women performed the rest of the work. Therefore, the lodge was considered owned by the women. The National Historic Park at Knife River shows the indentations of where the lodges once stood, but to get a feel for an active village one must visit the Fort Berthold Indian Reservation to see the only village to be constructed by Mandan, Hidatsa and Arikara Nations in over 100 years.

PORTOBELLO MUSHROOMS SCALLOP SALAD

2 pounds bay scallops
1 pound portobello mushrooms, sliced
½ teaspoon ground allspice
1 teaspoon ground coriander
1 teaspoon marjoram
1 teaspoon fine sea salt
3 cups shredded arugula
1 head romaine lettuce

1. Preheat broiler.
2. Arrange scallops and mushrooms on broiler pan; sprinkle with allspice, coriander, marjoram and salt.
3. Broil 5 to 6 minutes or until scallops are opaque.
4. Remove scallops and mushrooms from oven; drain. Transfer to cool platter and chill for 30 minutes.
5. Arrange arugula and romaine leaves on 6 chilled salad plates; add scallops and mushrooms.

Serves 6

SHRIMP SALAD

2 tablespoons fine sea salt
1 tablespoon cayenne pepper (optional)
1 tablespoon distilled white vinegar
2 pounds shrimp, shell on
½ cup mayonnaise
juice of 1 lemon
2 tablespoons red wine vinegar
¼ teaspoon hot sauce (optional)
2 hard-boiled eggs, chopped
¼ cup finely chopped celery
lettuce, thinly sliced avocado,
hard-boiled-egg halves and sliced grape
   tomatoes for garnish

1. In a 4-quart saucepan, combine 2½ quarts water, 2 tablespoons salt, the cayenne and white vinegar, and bring to a boil.
2. Add shrimp, let return to a boil and then turn off the heat. Let soak for 5 minutes in the cooking liquid; drain. When cool enough to handle, shell the shrimp.
3. In a bowl, blend together the mayonnaise, lemon juice, red wine vinegar and hot sauce. Stir in the shrimp, chopped eggs and celery. Season with salt to taste. Serve on lettuce leaves. Garnish with sliced avocado, hard-boiled egg and grape tomatoes if desired.

Serves 4 - 6

SAVIOR OF THE UNION
www.nps.gov/linc

"In this temple, as in the hearts of the people for whom he saved the Union, the memory of Abraham Lincoln is enshrined forever."

Even before the 16th President had passed away, there was talk about having a memorial dedicated to him. Abraham Lincoln was assassinated on April 14, 1865, just as the Civil War was ending. By March of 1867, Congress incorporated the Lincoln Monument Association to build a memorial to the slain 16th president. The land beneath the Memorial was not even there when Lincoln died. It wasn't until the Potomac was dredged and the mud was laid from the Washington Memorial to where it ends today that talks really began in earnest. Construction began in 1914 and the Memorial was finally dedicated in 1922. His Second Inaugural Address and his Gettyburg Address are engraved on the north and south walls of the building. In August, 1963, Martin Luther King Jr. gave his "I Have a Dream" speech, during the rally at the end of the March on Washington for Jobs and Freedom. This has always been my favorite Memorial building in D.C. and a visit to D.C. must include a visit to read the, "Four Score and Seven years ago.." speech.

MARINATED CUCUMBER SALAD

3 English cucumbers, thinly sliced
1 large red onion, thinly sliced
½ teaspoon fine sea salt
ice cubes
1-2 teaspoons sugar or sweetener
1½ cups white wine vinegar
2 tablespoons lemon juice
2 tablespoons olive oil
¼ teaspoon mustard seed
¼ teaspoon celery seed
1 teaspoon fine sea salt
freshly ground black pepper to taste

1. Peel the cucumbers then halve lengthwise. Scoop out the seeds then slice into ½-inch slices.
2. Peel and thinly slice the red onion and place in a 13 x 9-inch baking dish with the cucumber.
3. Sprinkle evenly with sea salt. Cover with ice. Place in refrigerator and chill 3 hours or until cool and crisp. Drain and return to dish.
4. Combine the vinegar, lemon juice, oil, sugar, spices, sea salt and pepper in a bowl and whisk together.
5. Pour mixture over cucumbers and red onion and mix well. Cover and chill at least 4 hours or up to 5 days. Serve cold.

Serves 4 - 6

Entrees

LINCOLN MEMORIAL

BRITISH FINALLY LOSE

www.nps.gov/gero

The British controlled the lands to the west of the Appalachian Mountain as a result of the French and Indian War. The Royal Proclamation of 1763 forbid the settlement of lands west of the Appalachians. For settlers who ignored the proclamation the British sent Indian war parties. Enter George Rogers Clark. Clark was not a military man, but a surveyor. Yet he organized the Kentucky militia to defend against these raids. He believed rather than wait for an attack, a major offensive campaign was needed. He took his plan to Patrick Henry, governor of Virginia, and gain approval. In the winter of 1779, Clark began a military campaign to retake Fort Sackville. It was a 210-mile, 18-day march with 170 men through a very cold winter. Clark ordered his men to display any and all American flags they had to create the illusion that he had more men than 170. He retook the Fort near Vincennes from Henry Hamilton, Lieutenant Governor of Canada. On the morning of February 25, 1779, the British flag would not be raised above the Fort.

TROPICAL PORK CHOPS

4 rib pork chops
¼ teaspoon fine sea salt
⅛ teaspoon freshly ground black pepper
½ cup unbleached all-purpose flour
1 can crushed pineapple, undrained
½ cup ketchup
¼ cup distilled white vinegar
2 tablespoons light-brown sugar
1 tablespoon soy sauce
1 tablespoon Worcestershire® sauce

1. Season pork chops on both sides with salt and pepper. Coat both sides in flour.
2. Heat oil in a large skillet. Brown chops for about 2 to 3 minutes per side, in batches if necessary.
3. Mix together pineapple, ketchup, vinegar, brown sugar, soy sauce, and Worcestershire sauce. Pour over chops.
4. Cook, covered, over low heat for about 30 minutes or until chops are tender. Add a little water, if necessary, during cooking if sauce becomes too thick. Serve with pilaf and green beans, if desired.

Serves 4

APPLE CRANBERRY PORK CHOPS

6 pork chops, boned or boneless
4 medium apples, peeled and sliced
¼ teaspoon thyme
¼ teaspoon nutmeg
3 large onions
1½ tablespoons brown sugar
2 tablespoons dried cranberries
1 bay leaf
1 cup beef stock

1. Preheat oven to 350 degrees.
2. Brown pork chops on both sides in stick-free pan.
3. Place one half of onion and apples in casserole. Put pork chops on top; add remaining onion and apple. Sprinkle brown sugar, thyme, nutmeg, cranberries and bay leaf on top. Pour beef stock over the apple and pork mixture.
4. Bake for one hour.

Serves 6

A REVOLUTION BEGINS – A NATION IS BORN

On April 18, 1775, Paul Revere got the signal of "two if by sea" and began his famous ride to let the colonist know that the British had landed. In the early morning hours of the 19th as the British marched west, they encountered 73 militia men and the "shot heard round the world" happened and the Revolutionary War began. The British marched on Concord, MA with orders to destroy the weapons and supplies that were stored there. Massachusetts Bay Colony relied upon a part-time citizen militia for its defense. All free men ages 16 to 60 were required to serve in their town's militia company and attend regular trainings. They were farmers, artisans, merchants, and laborers. Rich men and poor served, as did some African and Native Americans. In 1775 many towns had also recruited elite "minute companies," which became known as the minute men who were ready to march at a moment's warning, hence "minute men."

ORANGE ALMOND CHICKEN

½ cup dried cranberries
1 cup orange juice
1 cut-up broiler-fryer chicken
1 teaspoon fine sea salt
freshly ground black pepper
¼ cup butter
2 tablespoons flour
⅛ teaspoon cinnamon or nutmeg
dash ground ginger
1½ cups orange juice
1 cup orange sections
3 cups hot cooked rice

1. Soak dried cranberries in orange juice overnight. Drain juice.
2. Sprinkle chicken with salt and pepper.
3. Melt butter in large skillet, add chicken and brown over medium heat until golden brown. Remove from heat and place chicken on platter.
4. Add flour, cinnamon, and ginger to skillet and blend to make a smooth paste.
5. Gradually stir in orange juice; return to heat and bring to a boil, stirring constantly. Reduce heat; return chicken to pan and add almonds.
6. Cover and simmer 40 to 50 minutes or until tender. Add dried cranberries, orange sections and heat through.
7. Serve over hot cooked rice.

ROAST PORK LOIN WITH ORANGE JUICE

¾ cup orange juice
¾ teaspoon paprika
¾ teaspoon garlic powder
½ teaspoon onion powder
½ teaspoon dried oregano
½ teaspoon fine sea salt
½ teaspoon freshly ground black pepper
1 center-cut loin of pork on the bone
¾ cup white wine

1. Preheat oven to 450 degrees.
2. In a small bowl, combine paprika, garlic powder, onion powder, oregano, salt and pepper. Pat mixture over top of pork and place pork in a small, heavy roasting pan or heavy oven-safe skillet.
3. Roast 10 minutes. Reduce heat to 325 degrees and pour orange juice and wine around (not over) the pork. Roast until the pan juices run clear and a meat thermometer registers 160 degrees for medium, 1 to 1¼ hours.
4. Remove pork from oven and allow to rest 15 minutes in pan. There should be about ⅓ cup juices left in pan. If there are more, remove pork to a platter and cook juices over medium-low heat until reduced to ⅓ cup. Thinly slice pork and spoon pan juices over top.

Serves 4

JAEGERSCHNITZEL

4 boneless pork chops
½ pound bacon, chopped
2 cups cremini mushrooms, quartered
2 olive oil, plus more if necessary
½ cup flour, for dredging
2 large eggs, lightly beaten
1 cup bread crumbs
4 tablespoons butter
4 tablespoons flour
3 cups beef broth
fine sea salt to taste
freshly ground black pepper

1. Cut each pork chop in half through the middle to create two thinner pieces out of each chop. Place each pork chop in a zip-loc bag, and with a mallet, pound to flatten to about ¼-inch thick. Season each piece with a bit of salt. Then dredge the pork in the flour, dip in the lightly beaten eggs, and coat in the bread crumbs. Set the breaded chops aside.
2. In a large pan, over medium heat, cook the bacon until it just begins to get crispy, about 5 to 7 minutes. Use a slotted spoon to remove the bacon, leaving the rendered fat in the pan. Set the bacon aside.
3. Add the mushrooms to the bacon fat remaining in the pan and cook for 5 to 7 minutes over medium heat until the mushrooms are tender and lightly browned Use a slotted spoon to remove the mushrooms and set aside.
4. Add 1 to 2 tablespoons of olive oil to the bacon fat remaining in the pan, so that you have a very thin, even layer of bacon fat and oil. Add the breaded pork cutlets and cook for 2 to 3 minutes on each side, over medium heat, until they become lightly browned and cooked through. Set the cooked pork aside.
5. If the pan has any burned bits on the bottom, clean the pan before proceeding or use a new pan for the following steps.
6. Add butter and flour to the pan over medium heat. Whisk to combine. Cook for a minute or two. Then, gradually begin whisking in the beef stock. Bring to a simmer. Simmer for about 5 minutes, whisking frequently. The sauce will thicken. Season with salt and pepper, to taste.
7. Add the cooked pork cutlets, mushrooms, bacon, and any juices to the sauce. Gently move the pan to coat the pork in the sauce. Cook for a minute or two to reheat all components. Taste and adjust seasonings if necessary.
8. Serve with warm butter-sautéed spaetzle or German-style fried potatoes.

Serves 4

Cook's Note: Jägerschnitzel means "hunter's cutlets" in German. The Texas specialty chicken fried steak is believed to be an outgrowth of this dish brought to the USA by German immigrants.

PEACH STUFFED CHICKEN BREASTS

6 whole chicken breasts, skinned & boned
1½ teaspoons fine sea salt
⅛ teaspoon freshly ground pepper
3 fresh peaches, peeled & diced
½ cup chopped onion
½ cup coarsely chopped cashews
⅛ teaspoon ground ginger
½ cup butter
2 fresh peaches, peeled & sliced
1 (8-ounce) carton sour cream
½ cup brown sugar, firmly packed
2 teaspoons Dijon mustard
1 tablespoon brandy
¼ teaspoon fine sea salt

1. Preheat oven to 375 degrees.
2. Place each chicken breast on a sheet of waxed paper and flatten to ¼-inch. Sprinkle salt and pepper over inside of each breast; set aside.
3. Combine 3 fresh peaches, onions, cashews and ginger, stirring well. Place ¼ cup filling in center of each breast; fold side of chicken over filling and secure with toothpick.
4. Melt butter in a 13 x 9 x 2-inch baking pan; place breasts top side down in butter. Bake, covered for 25 minutes. Uncover, turn chicken and bake 20 minutes more.
5. Make peach sauce by combining 2 fresh peaches, sour cream, brown sugar, mustard, brandy and salt. Cook over low heat for 8 minutes. Serve with chicken breasts.

Serves 6

GATEWAY TO THE SOUTH
www.nps.gov/chch

In September 1863, Union and Confederate soldiers met at the Battle of Chickamauga which the Confederates won driving the Union forces out of southeastern Tennessee and northwestern Georgia. It was the second costliest battle, behind Gettysburg, of the Civil War. By November 1863, fighting renewed and was occurring at Missionary Ridge and Lookout Mountain. This became known as the Battle of Chattanooga and it was a significant win for the north. Chattanooga was an important railroad hub and by controlling it, Union forces were able to use it as a gateway to other campaigns in the south. After the fighting, a Confederate soldier ominously wrote, "This...is the death-knell of the Confederacy."

SOUTHERN FRIED CHICKEN

3 cups buttermilk, divided
3 teaspoons fine sea salt, divided
1 teaspoon freshly ground pepper, divided
1 broiler/fryer chicken (3 to 4 pounds), cut up
vegetable oil for deep-fat frying
2 cups all-purpose flour

1. In a shallow bowl, combine 2 cups buttermilk, 1 teaspoon salt and ⅛ teaspoon pepper. Pour mixture in zip-lock plastic bag. Add chicken a few pieces at a time; turn to coat. Refrigerate overnight.
2. In an electric skillet or deep fryer, heat oil to 375 degrees.
3. Meanwhile, place remaining buttermilk in a shallow bowl. In another shallow bowl, whisk flour and remaining salt and pepper.
4. Place half of flour mixture in another shallow bowl (for a second coat of breading). Drain chicken, discarding marinade; pat chicken dry. Dip in flour mixture to coat both sides; shake off excess. Dip in buttermilk, allowing excess to drain off. For the second coat of breading, dip chicken in remaining flour mixture, patting to help coating adhere.
5. Fry chicken, a few pieces at a time, 4 to 5 minutes on each side or until browned and juices run clear. Drain on paper towels.

Serves 6

WHERE THE CIVIL WAR BEGAN
www.nps.gov/fosu

Confederates fired the first shots of the Civil War upon Federal troops at Fort Sumter at 4:30 a.m. on April 12, 1861. Ft. Sumter is located in Charleston Harbor, South Carolina. The fort was under the command of U.S. Major Robert Anderson when it was bombarded by Confederate General P.G.T. Beauregard and his troops. After 34 hours of constant artillery attack, Anderson surrendered along with 86 men. It took the Union four years before the Confederates abandoned the Fort and they retook it. Besides its roll in the Civil War, it was built on Gadsden's Wharf where hundreds of thousands of enslaved Africans were brought into the United States. It only seems fitting that this is where the Civil War began.

CHICKEN STOLTZUS
Groff's Farm Restaurant • Mt. Joy

1 (5-pound) roasting chicken, giblets removed
1½ quarts water
1 tablespoon fine sea salt
⅓ teaspoon freshly ground black pepper
pinch of saffron
1½ sticks butter
¾ cup all-purpose flour
1 cup half and half
¼ cup finely chopped fresh parsley or
2 tablespoons dried parsley
1 (2 sticks) cup butter
3 cups all-purpose flour
1 teaspoon fine sea salt
about ½ cup ice water

1. Place chicken in a 6-quart pot and add water, salt, pepper and saffron; bring to a boil. Reduce heat and simmer, partially covered, for 1 hour. Remove chicken and let cool. Debone chicken, remove skin and cut into bite-sized pieces. Strain the stock through a double thickness of cheese-cloth and reduce it over high heat until it makes 4 cups.
2. Melt 1½ sticks butter in original pot and whisk in flour over medium heat to make a roux. Cook until bubbling and golden. Slowly whisk in the stock and cream, stirring constantly until smooth, creamy, and thickened, about 10 minutes. Add the chicken and parsley and heat thoroughly.
3. To make the pastry squares, first preheat oven to 350 degrees.
4. Cut 2 sticks butter into the flour with two knives or a pastry blender until coarse crumbs are formed.
5. Sprinkle ice water over crumbs with one hand while tossing them lightly with the other. Use only enough water to hold the dough together. Press the dough into a ball and turn it out onto a lightly floured surface. Divide into 2 or 3 parts. Roll each part to ¼-thick. Cut dough into 1-inch squares and bake on ungreased cookie sheets in oven for 12-15 minutes, until light brown.
6. Arrange the pastry squares on a heated platter and pour the chicken on top. (Make sure to leave the edges of the pastry squares showing.) Garnish with parsley sprigs.
7. Serve immediately or the pastry will become soggy.

Serves 6 – 8

Cooks Note: I first had this meal at Betty Groff's home in the early 80s and it was delicious. I have always remembered the meal and the atmosphere. She normally served dessert of chocolate cake and cracker pudding first because there would be "no room" for dessert.

APRICOT-GLAZED ROCK CORNISH HENS

6 Rock Cornish hens
fine sea salt to taste
freshly ground pepper to taste
2 tablespoons chopped fresh rosemary
1 cup dried apricot halves
1 cup unsweetened applesauce
1½ cups dry white wine
¼ cup brown sugar
finely grated zest of 1 orange
½ teaspoon ground cloves
fresh rosemary sprigs for garnish

1. Preheat oven to 350 degrees.
2. Rinse the hens inside and out under cold running water and pat dry. Season inside and out with salt and pepper. Truss the birds and place them, breast side up, in a roasting pan. Sprinkle the hens all over with the rosemary. Roast the birds 1 hour.
3. Meanwhile, prepare the apricot glaze. Quarter the dried apricots and combine with the applesauce and wine in a saucepan. Stir in the brown sugar, orange zest, and cloves. Simmer covered, stirring occasionally, for 30 minutes.
4. Press the glaze through a sieve or food mill, then spoon over the roasting game hens. Roast the birds until tender, 25 to 30 minutes. Serve garnished with fresh rosemary.

Serves 6

FORGOTTEN NATIONAL PARK

The second U.S. national park created is no longer a national park. Mackinac National Park in Michigan was established in 1875 and was returned to the state in 1895. It is now one of Michigan's State Parks. Most of Mackinac Island was already federal property, and the park itself was small. Most importantly, Congress gave the park to the War Department to administer. That meant that soldiers from the Fort Mackinac garrison could be used for the requisite operation and policing of the park. Mackinac National Park lasted just 20 years. In the 1890s the Army proposed to abandon Fort Mackinac, an action that would leave the park without a custodian. Alarmed at the prospect, Michigan governor John T. Rich petitioned Congress to turn the park over to the state of Michigan. This was done in 1895. Mackinac Island State Park, reportedly the first state-operated park in this country to be officially titled a "state park," remains a Michigan state park to this day.

Source: www.nationalparkstraveler.org

CHICKEN FRIED STEAK

1½ cups buttermilk
1 large egg, beaten
2 teaspoons fine sea salt
1 teaspoon freshly ground black pepper
1 cup all-purpose flour
1 teaspoon onion or garlic powder
1 pound cube steaks
2 tablespoons unsalted butter
1 cup beef broth
canola oil for frying

1. Whisk together buttermilk, egg, 1 teaspoon sea salt and ½ teaspoon pepper; place in a one-gallon zipper-locking bag with cubed steaks. Marinate refrigerated for at least 4 hours, overnight preferred.
2. Whisk together flour, remaining salt and pepper, and onion/garlic powder. Place in a shallow baking dish; reserve 2 tablespoons of seasoned flour for gravy later.
3. Transfer steaks and buttermilk marinade to a second shallow baking dish. Pull steaks from liquid and dredge each in flour, return to buttermilk mixture, then back into flour, making sure to work the seasoned flour into the steak by pressing with your fingertips. Place steaks on a wire rack or paper towels on a sheet pan and refrigerate 30 minutes.
4. Add oil to a deep skillet, Dutch oven or deep fryer making sure to only come up about half way to the top of the pan; heat oil to 350 degrees to 375 degrees. Working in batches, fry breaded steaks for 3 to 4 minutes on each side. Place steaks on a paper towel or rack to drain; keep warm.
5. Melt butter in a saucepan over medium-high heat; add reserved seasoned flour. Whisk for 3 minutes or until flour just begins to brown; pour in broth while constantly whisking. Bring gravy to a boil then reduce to a simmer while whisking for 3 minutes.
6. Serve steaks topped with warm gravy, mashed potatoes, green beans and homemade biscuits.

Serves 4 - 6

SACRED PIPES
www.nps.gov/pipe

We all remember seeing Western movies that show a Native American smoking a peace pipe. Well more than likely those pipes were made from the rock at Pipestone National Monument in Minnesota. These lands are sacred to many American tribes who still today quarry the rocks to make pipestones for prayer ceremonies. The park was established by Congress in 1937, to preserve the quarries for future generations. It is believed that digging at the site began in the 17th century. This pipestone was favored by the Plains tribes, but by the 1700 it is thought that the Dakota Sioux controlled the quarries.

TURKEY AND CRANBERRY HASH

2 tablespoons (¼ stick) unsalted butter
1 onion, finely chopped
1 celery rib, finely chopped
1 pound cooked skinless turkey, white and dark meat combined, cut into ½-inch cubes
½ cup chopped fresh cranberries or ¼ cup dried cranberries soaked in white wine
¼ cup leftover turkey gravy or heavy cream
fine sea salt to taste
freshly ground black pepper to taste
snipped fresh chives, for garnish

1. In a large skillet with sloping sides over medium-high heat, melt the butter. Add the onion and celery. Cook, stirring often, until softened, 3-5 minutes.
2. Add the turkey, cranberries, and gravy. Season with salt and pepper and reduce the heat to medium.
3. Cover and cook until the bottom of chicken is crusty brown, 20-25 minutes. Slip out onto a plate and carefully flip to the other side.
4. Cook, uncovered, until golden brown on the other side, about 15 minutes. Slide out onto a work surface and sprinkle with chives.
5. Cut into wedges and serve.

Serves 6 - 8

Source: The Colonial Williamsburg Tavern Cookbook

POCAHONTAS AND CAPTAIN JOHN SMITH

www.nps.gov/jame

In school we all learned about the tale involving Pocahontas and English Captain John Smith. However, history tells us a different story. Pocahontas was the last child of the acknowledged paramount chief, Powhatan. He was the chief of as many as 30 tribes, with more than 150 towns. Powhatan met the English when he was in his 60s in 1607. Originally, the relationship between them was cordial with Powhatan believing that peace would be better for the tribes under his power. In December 1607, Captain Smith was captured by Powhatan's men. Later in his life, he claimed that Pocahontas had saved him, but historians question that as she would have been quite young (8-11). Maybe he felt it made the story more interesting. Powhatan and the English became allies and trading partners in early 1608. It is felt that the food provided by Powhatan helped the English survive the their first winter in Jamestown. Even with the food assistance more than half of the settlers died that first winter.

KENTUCKY HOT BROWN

www.brownhotel.com

Developed in 1920s by Chef Fred Schmidt at the Brown Hotel in Louisville, Kentucky and enjoyed worldwide by millions.

1½ tablespoons salted butter
1½ tablespoons all-purpose flour
1½ cups heavy cream
¼ cup Pecorino Romano cheese, plus extra for garnish
pinch of ground nutmeg
fine sea salt
freshly ground black pepper
14 ounces sliced roasted turkey breast, sliced thick
4 slices of Texas toast (crusts trimmed)
4 slices of cooked bacon
2 Roma tomatoes, sliced in half
paprika
parsley

1. In a two-quart saucepan, melt butter and slowly whisk in flour until combined to form a thick paste or roux. Continue to cook roux for 2 minutes over medium-low heat, stirring frequently. Whisk heavy cream into the roux and cook over medium heat until the cream begins to simmer, about 2 to 3 minutes. Remove sauce from heat and slowly whisk in Pecorino-Romano cheese until the Mornay sauce is smooth. Add nutmeg, salt and pepper to taste.
2. For each Hot Brown, place two slices of toast in an oven safe dish and cover each with half of the turkey breast. Take the two halves of Roma tomato and two toast points and set them alongside the base of each turkey and toast. Pour half of the sauce over each sandwich, completely covering it. Sprinkle with additional cheese. Place entire dish under a broiler until cheese begins to brown and bubble. Remove and cross two pieces of crispy bacon on top. Sprinkle with paprika and parsley and serve immediately.

Source: Brown Hotel

Powhatan retired from being chief in 1616. Pocahontas had gone to Great Britain with her husband, John Rolfe and son. When it came time to return, she got sick and passed away in 1617 and was buried in Great Britain. Her father died shortly after in 1618 and the "Peace of Pocahontas" began to unravel. Life for her people would never be the same.

MARINATED BEEF TENDERLOIN

¼ cup lemon juice
½ cup soy sauce
½ cup vegetable oil
½ cup brown sugar
1 tablespoon minced ginger
3 tablespoons minced garlic
2 teaspoons dry mustard
½ teaspoon fine sea salt
¼ teaspoon freshly ground black pepper
3 pounds beef tenderloin, trimmed

1. In a bowl, combine wine, lemon juice, soy sauce, oil, brown sugar, ginger, garlic, mustard, salt and pepper.
2. Add beef and marinate for at least 3 hours in refrigerator, turning beef in marinade several times.
3. Prepare a charcoal or gas grill and grill beef to desired doneness. Allow tenderloin to rest 20 minutes before slicing.

Serves 6 - 8

The Bush Family Cookbook

WHAT IS A BIOSPHERE RESERVE?

When we think of a National Park, we think mountains, monuments, seashores, and battlefields. We do not think swamps or old growth bottomland hardwood forests. When is a swamp not a swamp? Congaree National Park is not a swamp because there is no standing water for most of the year. Waters from the Congaree and Wateree Rivers sweep through the floodplain, carrying nutrients and sediments that nourish and rejuvenate this ecosystem and support the growth of national and state champion trees. People have been using the floodplain for many purposes for over 13,000 years, long before it became a national park. While water has been an enduring force that has shaped this landscape, humans have left their mark as well. From prehistoric natives to Spanish explorers, Revolutionary War patriots to escaped slaves, loggers and conservationists, this forest landscape is rich in the stories of the people who have called it both a home and a refuge and have helped to make it what it is today. In 1983, Congaree National Park was designated by UNESCO an International Biosphere Reserve.

STEAK AND BOURSIN SANDWICHES

1 (1-pound) piece flank steak
¾ teaspoon fine sea salt
½ teaspoon freshly ground black pepper
1 (24-inch-long) baguette or 4 (6-inch-long) ciabatta rolls
1 package Boursin cheese
2 tablespoons olive oil
2 hearts of romaine, halved lengthwise

1. Preheat broiler.
2. Pat steak dry and sprinkle all over with salt and pepper. Put on rack of a broiler pan and broil 2 to 3 inches from heat, turning over once, 6 to 8 minutes total for medium-rare. Transfer to a cutting board and let stand 5 minutes.
3. While steak broils, cut baguette into 4 sections, then halve each horizontally. Spread Boursin over bottom halves of bread.
4. While steak stands, heat 1 tablespoon oil in a 12-inch heavy skillet over moderately high heat until hot but not smoking, then sauté romaine in 2 batches, turning over once, until browned in spots and slightly wilted, about 2 minutes per batch. Add remaining tablespoon oil to skillet between batches. Transfer as sautéed to cutting board with meat. Cut off and discard core end of romaine, then lay romaine on top of Boursin.
5. Cut steak across the grain into thin slices and divide among sandwiches.

Makes 4 servings.

Cook's Note: Boursin now comes in a variety of flavors such as maple bourbon or cranberry. Changes throughout the year. Give you roast beef sandwiches a new flavor, you won't regret it

BIRTHPLACE OF THE AMERICAN INDUSTRIAL REVOLUTION

The Blackstone River Valley of Massachusetts and Rhode Island is the "Birthplace of the American Industrial Revolution," the place where America made the transformation from farm to factory. America's first textile mill could have been built along practically any river on the eastern seaboard, but in 1790 the forces of capital, ingenuity, mechanical know-how and skilled labor came together at Pawtucket, Rhode Island where the Blackstone River provided the power that kicked off America's drive to industrialization.

VEAL SCALLOPINI

¼ cup extra virgin olive oil
6 veal cutlets, pounded thin, about 6 to 8 minutes
1 cup all-purpose flour for dredging
fine sea salt to taste
freshly ground black pepper to taste
½ cup dry white wine
2 tablespoons freshly squeezed lemon
2 tablespoons butter
1 tablespoon small capers
1 tablespoon Italian flat-leafed parsley, chopped for garnish

1. Prepare a large nonstick sauté pan coated with olive oil over medium heat. Lightly pound the cutlets with a mallet or rolling pin between sheets of wax paper and flatten to uniform thickness.
2. Dip cutlets in flour or shake a few at a time in a zip-loc bag. Sauté cutlets seasoned with salt and pepper until lightly browned, about 2 minutes on each side.
3. Add the wine, lemon juice, butter and capers; simmer, turning cutlets until cooked through, about 10 minutes.
4. Place the medallions topped with lemon caper sauce and garnish with parsley.

Serves 6

CRANBERRY SHORT RIBS

1½ pounds bone-in beef short ribs
½ teaspoon fine sea salt, divided
¼ teaspoon freshly ground black pepper
1 tablespoon all-purpose flour
1 tablespoon brown sugar
⅛ teaspoon ground mustard
dash ground cloves
¾ cup cranberry wine
2 teaspoons cider vinegar
½ cup fresh or frozen cranberries
1½ to 2 teaspoons grated lemon zest

1. Preheat oven to 350 degrees.
2. Spray an 8-inch square baking dish with Pam or olive oil. Place ribs in the baking dish; sprinkle ribs with ¼ teaspoon salt and pepper. Bake, covered, until tender, about 1¼ to 1½ hours.
3. In a small saucepan, combine flour, brown sugar, mustard, cloves and remaining sea salt; gradually whisk in wine and vinegar until smooth. Stir in cranberries, lemon zest and bring to a boil. Cook and stir until thickened, about 2 minutes.
4. Drain ribs. Pour cranberry mixture over ribs.
5. Bake, uncovered, 15 minutes longer.

Serves 2

DANCING FIREFLIES

Great Smoky Mountains National Park is the most visited national park with more than 11 million guests per year. The Park was established in 1934 and are called the Smokies due to the ever-present morning fog. There are about 100 species of trees that are native to the Smokies—more than any other national park in North America. It is also home to over 1,500 types of flowering plants that bloom year-round. A Spring Wildflower Pilgrimage takes places each year, a festival with many guided walks and hikes. One of the country's greatest light shows occurs in late April and early May when millions of synchronous fireflies take flight. Their light patterns are part of their mating display. Each species of firefly has a characteristic flash pattern that helps its male and female individuals recognize each other. Most species produce a greenish-yellow light; one species has a bluish light. The males fly and flash and the usually stationary females respond with a flash. The production of light by living organisms is called bioluminescence.

MARINATED SWORDFISH

2½ pounds swordfish, ¾-inch thick, preferably in 1 piece
freshly ground black pepper
4 tablespoons butter, cut in 1-inch pieces
3 tablespoons fresh chives, chopped
2 tablespoons fresh basil, chopped
1 tablespoon fresh oregano, chopped
1 tablespoon fresh dill, chopped
2 tablespoons fresh flat-leafed parsley, chopped
½ cup light soy sauce

1. Several hours before you want to serve the fish, place it in an ovenproof baking dish, season with fresh pepper and dot with butter. Sprinkle with chopped herbs and pour the soy sauce over the top. Cover with plastic wrap and refrigerate.
2. One hour before you are going to cook it, remove the fish from the refrigerator and let it stand at room temperature.
3. Heat the broiler, then place the fish in the marinade, under it. Broil on one side only for about 10 minutes, basting often to keep the fish moist. It is ready when the skin around the outside pulls away from the flesh easily.

Serves 6

FINNAN HADDIE "GRAY GULL"

2 pounds loin end of haddock
4 tablespoons butter
4 tablespoons flour
¼ teaspoon fine sea salt
⅛ teaspoon freshly ground pepper
2 cups milk
½ teaspoon prepared mustard
2 tablespoons sherry
¾ cup grated sharp cheddar cheese

1. Preheat oven to 325 degrees.
2. Cook fish in boiling water until it will flake, about 5 minutes; drain.
3. Make sauce of remaining ingredients, reserving a little of the cheese for the top of casserole.
4. Add flaked fish to same, mixing gently. Place mixture in a buttered casserole.
5. Add remaining cheese and some dry bread crumbs if desired.
6. Bake until mixture bubbles. Serve with baked potato.

Serves 4

SWORDFISH AND PECANS

5 tablespoons butter, melted
1 cup cracker crumbs
1 large swordfish steak
½ lemon, juiced, rind reserved
½ lime, juiced, rind reserved
½ cup pecan halves

1. Preheat oven to 425 degrees.
2. Melt butter in a small skillet. In a small bowl, combine cracker crumbs with just enough melted butter to moisten. Spread mixture over swordfish.
3. Bake for 20-25 minutes, or until it flakes.
4. Meanwhile, add lemon and lime juices and both rinds to rest of melted butter in skillet. Add pecans. Heat over lowest heat for 10 minutes. Do not allow to bubble and keep browning to a minimum. Remove rinds. Place fish on a serving platter and pour pecan mixture over all.

Serves 2 - 4

CRABMEAT SCAMPI

4 tablespoons olive oil
4 tablespoons butter, cut into pieces
2 tablespoons chopped garlic
½ teaspoon dried red pepper
4 teaspoons Worcestershire® sauce
2 tablespoons fresh lemon juice
⅔ cup white wine
1 pound jumbo lump crabmeat, picked over for shells
1 teaspoon chopped fresh parsley
fine sea salt
freshly ground black pepper
1 pound cooked pasta, or
4 cups cooked rice

1. Heat the oil and butter in a large skillet over medium heat.
2. Add the garlic and cook until lightly golden.
3. Add the red pepper, Worcestershire sauce®, lemon juice, and white wine. Bring to a boil and cook for 4 minutes.
4. Gently stir in the crabmeat and parsley. Season with salt and pepper to taste.
5. Serve over pasta or rice.

Serves 4

Coastal Cooking with John Shields

CRAB CRUST SCROD

½ cup mayonnaise
¾ cup crabmeat
½ cup grated Parmesan cheese
2 tablespoons chopped parsley
6 ounces white wine
4 scrod fillets

1. Preheat oven to 450 degrees.
2. Mix mayonnaise, crabmeat, Parmesan cheese and parsley in a bowl. Stir in small amount of white wine until mixture is of a spreadable consistency.
3. Place the fillets in a baking dish; pour remaining wine over the top. Spread with crab mixture.
4. Bake for 7 minutes or until the fish flakes and crust is brown.

Serves 4

SHRIMP PO' BOY

2½ teaspoons fine sea salt
1 teaspoon cayenne pepper
1 teaspoon garlic powder
1 teaspoon paprika
½ teaspoon dried oregano
½ teaspoon dried thyme
½ teaspoon freshly ground black pepper
½ teaspoon onion powder
vegetable oil for frying
1½ pounds medium shrimp, peeled & deveined
1 cup buttermilk
1½ cups all-purpose flour
1 cup cornmeal
4 (8"- long) French baguette rolls, split horizontally
Rémoulade sauce (page 117)
sliced tomatoes (Creole tomatoes if possible)
dill pickles
hot sauce (optional)

1. Combine first 8 ingredients in bowl.
2. Add vegetable oil to heavy wide pot to a depth of 2 inches. Heat over medium heat to 350 degrees.
3. While oil is heating, place shrimp and 2 tablespoons spice mix in a medium bowl and toss to coat.
4. In a second bowl, pour buttermilk. In a third bowl whisk flour and cornmeal.
5. Dip seasoned shrimp briefly in buttermilk, then coat with flour mixture. Working in batches, fry shrimp, stirring occasionally, until golden brown and just cooked through, about 4 minutes per batch. Transfer to paper towels to drain.
6. Open rolls and spread cut sides with rémoulade. Top with lettuce, tomato, pickles, and shrimp. Serve with hot sauce, if desired.

Cook's Note: Po boys originated in New Orleans during the transit strike in 1929 by the Martin brothers who jokingly referred to their former co-workers as "Poor Boys" which became "Po boys." It can be made with shrimp, fish, crab and even poultry. Remember make sure the oil is hot enough so the shrimp don't soak up more oil.

PEOPLE OF POVERTY POINT

www.nps.gov/popo

Over 3000 years ago (between 1700 and 1100 B.C.), a forgotten culture at Poverty Point, Louisiana developed an extensive trading network that covered the eastern half of the United States. The inhabitants of the Point built a complex of earthen mounds and ridges that involved moving over 70 tons of rocks and soil and over 5 million hours of labor to complete. Materials for the construction came from the Ozark Mountains and the Ohio and Tennessee River Valley. Soapstone for vessels came from the Appalachian foothills of northern Alabama and Georgia. Other materials came from distant places in the Eastern United States. While archaeologist feels thousands of people lived at The Point, they left behind only artifacts, but they didn't leave behind such as burials and crop remains. While burial mounds were common throughout the southeastern and central U.S., the absence of human remains suggests that these monumental earthworks were being used for other purposes. It has never been determined why the site was abandoned.

STEAMED MUSSELS IN WINE AND GARLIC

3 tablespoons chopped garlic
2 yellow onions, chopped
1 stick butter
2 bay leaves
1 tablespoon oregano
1 tablespoon parsley
1½ cups white wine
4 pounds fresh mussels or hard-shell clams

1. Sauté onions and garlic in butter until lightly browned.
2. Add bay leaves, spices, and white wine; cook to reduce by half.
3. Add mussels or clams.
4. Cover and cook until shells open about three to four minutes.
5. Serve with angel hair pasta or with artisan bread.

Serves 4

BROILED CAPE SCALLOPS

4 broccoli crowns
3 pounds Cape or bay scallops
½ pound butter
juice of 1 lemon
1 cup bread crumbs
1 tablespoon parsley, minced
¼ teaspoon ground thyme
fine sea salt to taste
freshly ground white pepper to taste
paprika

1. Preheat broiler.
2. Dry scallops in paper towels.
3. Melt butter in heavy, broiler-proof casserole. Add lemon juice and scallops. Mix well until all scallops are evenly coated. Lay scallops out in one layer.
4. Mix bread crumbs with parsley, thyme, salt, and pepper. Scatter crumbs on top and sprinkle scallops with paprika.
5. Broil 6-inches from top of broiler until just cooked through about 10 to 15 minutes. Do not overcook.
6. Serve at once, garnished with parsley sprig and lemon juice.

Serves 6

Cook's Note: The season officially opens on November 1st and lasts through the beginning of March, depending on the supply, which varies from season to season. Genuine Cape Scallops are not referred to as "Bays," so be very careful. Genuine Capes are from Cape Cod, usually around Chatham, Martha's Vineyard and Nantucket.

A PARK OF MANY CHOICES
www.nps.gov/sari

Imagine a ballgame that is over 3500 years old. Mesoamerican ballgame has been played by the pre-Columbian people of Ancient Mesoamerica. Salt River Bay is a living museum on St. Croix, U.S. Virgin Islands. The park preserves prehistoric and colonial-era archeological sites, including the only existing example of a ball court in the US Virgin Islands. Besides preserving ancient history, the Park is a vital ecosystem of mangroves, estuary, coral reefs, and a submarine canyon. The Park is known for two special things, first the landing of Christopher Columbus in November, 1493 and the other is its bioluminescent bay. The glowing water of the Bio Bay is created by micro-organism and bioluminescent marine life including comb-jellies or Fireworms. Bio Bays are very rare with only seven lagoons in the entire Caribbean region. Congress created the Park in 1992, but the Columbus landing site had already been designated a National Historic Landmark on October 9, 1960.

THE BEGINNING OF THE END

On April 9, 1865, the surrender of the Army of Northern Virginia in the McLean House in the village of Appomattox Court House, Virginia signaled the end of the nation's Civil War. Generals Robert E Lee and Ulysses S Grant signed the surrender at the home of Wilmer McLean. McLean had showed Lee's aides a few places which they rejected so he offered them his home. Lee arrived first and within the hour Grant appeared. The Generals were courteous to each other and engaged in small talk for about 30 minutes. The subject of surrender had not been discussed until finally, Lee, feeling the anguish of defeat, brought Grant's attention to it. Grant, who later confessed to being embarrassed at having to ask for the surrender from Lee, said simply that the terms would be just as he had outlined them in a previous letter. Grant treated the soldiers of the Confederacy with respect allowing them to return home with their mounts. Lee mentioned that his men had been without rations for several days, Grant arranged for 25,000 rations to be sent to the hungry Confederates. The character of both Lee and Grant was of such a high order that the surrender of the Army of Northern Virginia has been called "The Gentlemen's Agreement."

GRILLED STRIPED BASS WITH GARLIC AND BASIL

2 pounds striped bass fillet
3 tablespoons olive oil
juice of 1 lemon
4 - 6 tablespoons butter
4 cloves garlic, finely chopped
2 tablespoons basil, thinly chopped
dash of cayenne pepper

1. Marinate the fish in the oil and lemon juice for at least 30 minutes before grilling. Grill for 10 to 15 minutes, turning once. The length of time depends upon the thickness of the fillet.
2. Heat the butter in a saucepan and sauté the garlic for about 3 minutes, stirring frequently. Do not let it brown. Add the basil and a dash of cayenne pepper. Remove the pan from the heat.
3. Either pour the garlic butter over the fish just before serving or serve it in a sauceboat on the side.

Serves 4

COQUILLE SAINT JACQUES

1 pound fresh sea scallops
1 cup dry white wine
3 shallots, diced
¼ cup butter
1 pound shrimp, cooked and cleaned
1 pound cooked lobster
½ pound fresh mushrooms, sliced
¼ cup butter
1 tablespoon chives, chopped
1 tablespoon parsley, chopped
1 tablespoon brandy
1 teaspoon ground ginger
cayenne pepper, to taste
1 tablespoon fine sea salt
1 tablespoon dry mustard
1 quart light cream
4 tablespoons corn starch, moistened
3 eggs, lightly beaten

1. Poach scallops in wine for 5 minutes. At the same time sauté shallots in butter until transparent. Add shrimp and lobster to shallots.
2. In another pan sauté ½ pound fresh mushrooms in butter. To this add chives and parsley. When mushrooms are cooked add 1 tablespoon brandy and flambé mixture.
3. Add scallops to lobster and shrimp mixture. Season with ground ginger and a few grains of cayenne pepper, salt and dry mustard.
4. Scald light cream and thicken with 4 tablespoons moistened corn starch and cook until thick. Slowly add eggs to cream and then add mushrooms and cook for 5 minutes over low heat, stirring constantly.
5. Fold this sauce into fish mixture. Place in large casserole or individual ramekins. Cover with grated Parmesan cheese and brown under broiler.

Serves 6 - 8

ABRAHAM LINCOLN AND TEDDY ROOSEVELT HAVE THE MOST SITES NAMED FOR THEM:

- Abraham Lincoln Birthplace National Historic Site (Kentucky)
- Lincoln Memorial (D.C.)
- Lincoln Boyhood National Memorial (Indiana)
- Lincoln Home National Historic Site (Illinois)
- Theodore Roosevelt Island (D.C.)
- Theodore Roosevelt Birthplace National Historic Site (New York)
- Theodore Roosevelt Inaugural National Historic Site (New York)
- Theodore Roosevelt National Park (North Dakota)

A PIRATE AND A GENERAL
www.nps.gov/jela

Jean Laffite (or Lafitte) was born somewhere between 1776 in either France or the French territories of Saint-Domingue (now Tahiti). He was the most notorious and successful pirate that sailed the Gulf of Mexico and Caribbean. Laffite's privateers preyed on Spanish ships in particular as he had a deep seeded dislike of them. He then disposed of its plunder through merchants on the mainland. During the War of 1812, the British offered him a position in the Royal Navy which he declined. He then offered his services to General Andrew Jackson if he and his men were given pardons. He provided weapons and it is said he cannons were able to be of assistance to the U.S. Army. Jackson commended Laffite and said, "he was one of the ablest men" during the Battle of New Orleans. President James Madison issued a full pardon to Laffite and his men.

KEY LIME BAKED SNAPPER

1½ pounds red snapper fillets or other firm white fish
2 tablespoons Key Lime juice
1 tablespoon butter, melted
1½ teaspoons grated Key Lime peel
fine sea salt to taste
freshly ground black pepper
pinch nutmeg
fresh parsley, chopped
Key Limes wedges

1. Preheat oven to 350 degrees.
2. Cut snapper fillets into 6 serving-size pieces.
3. Combine the Key Lime juice, butter, Key Lime peel, salt, black pepper and nutmeg.
4. Mix thoroughly, then spoon over fish to cover completely.
5. Bake uncovered, basting with pan juices until the fish flakes easily, about 15 minutes or even less for very thin fillets.
6. Garnish fish with fresh parsley sprigs and lime wedges.

Serves 4

LOBSTER POPOVER

DeWolf Tavern · Bristol, RI · www.dewolfetavern.com

2 (1¼ pound) live lobsters
⅔ cup milk
1 large egg, beaten
1 teaspoon fine sea salt
6 tablespoons + 1 teaspoon all-purpose flour
2½ tablespoons Wondra® flour
2 tablespoons unsalted butter
6 medium shallots, minced
3 cloves garlic, minced
⅓ cup tomato paste
½ cup sherry
1 cup lobster or fish stock
2 tablespoons heavy cream
fine sea salt to taste
a few grains of fresh ground black pepper

1. Drop the lobsters into boiling salted water and cook for 7 minutes. Remove from the water and drain. When cool enough to handle, crack the shells and remove the meat. Cut the meat into 1½-inch pieces and drain well.
2. While the lobsters are cooking prepare the popovers. Whisk together the milk and egg. Combine the salt and both flours. Prepare the popover pan by spraying it with non-stick oil.
3. Combine milk, egg and salt and add to the dry mixture and mix together until just combined. Spoon into the popover pan, filling each cup no more than half full and place the pan into a cold oven. Turn the heat to 375 degrees and cook until browned and puffed, about 25-35 minutes.
4. Prepare the sauce by melting the butter in a medium saucepan. Add the shallots and garlic and cook over medium heat, stirring oven, until caramelized.
5. Add the tomato paste and continue cooking, stirring, until the tomato paste is caramelized as well.
6. Add the sherry and stock; whisk to combine. Finish with the cream, salt and pepper and cook the sauce until a light sauce-like consistency. Warm the lobster meat in the sauce.
7. To serve, cut a warm popover in half, place cut side up on a plate and spoon the lobster meat and sauce into the popover. Serve with a salad.

Serves 4

Chef's Note: Chef Sai says the trick for light and crisp popovers is the use of Wondra® flour and by beginning the baking in a cold oven.

A NEW BIRTH OF FREEDOM

www.nps.gov/ever/index.htm

"Four score and seven years ago our fathers brought forth on this continent, a new nation, conceived in Liberty, and dedicated to the proposition that all men are created equal."

Abraham Lincoln, Gettysburg Address, 1863

President Lincoln gave this famous two-minute address at the dedication of the Soldiers National Cemetery in Gettysburg, Pennsylvania. There were a total of 51,112 casulties during the three day battle. Of that 23,049 were Union and 28.063 were Confederate. General Robert E. Lee led his Army of Northern Virginia into Union territory in the hopes of a victory which could turn the tide of the War. Instead, his troops suffered a tragic lost and he had to retreat back to Virginia. The Battle of Gettysburg was a turning point of the Civil War.

LINGUINI WITH SHRIMP AND BROCCOLI

1 pound linguini
½ cup olive oil
2 tablespoons butter
3 large cloves of garlic, minced
1½ pounds shrimp, deveined, shelled
1 (16-ounce) package frozen chopped broccoli, thawed
3 tablespoons butter
¾ teaspoon freshly ground white pepper
⅓ cup grated Parmesan cheese

1. Cook the pasta al dente using the package directions, rinse with hot water and set aside.
2. Heat the olive oil and 2 tablespoons butter in a Dutch oven until the butter sizzles but does not smoke. Add the garlic and sauté until light golden brown.
3. Add the shrimp and sauté for 3 minutes or until the shrimp turn pink. Drain the broccoli well and add to the shrimp mixture. Cook for 1 minute, stirring constantly.
4. Add the pasta, 3 tablespoons butter, pepper and Parmesan cheese. Toss until well mixed and the pasta are heated to serving temperature.
5. Pour onto a heated serving platter and arrange in an attractive manner. Serve immediately.

Serves 8

Desserts

GETTYSBURG

FOUR FACES ON THE MOUNTAIN
www.nps.gov/moru

Four of our nations great leaders can be found on the side of a mountain in the Black Hills of South Dakota. The faces include those of George Washington, Thomas Jefferson, Abraham Lincoln and Theodore Roosevelt. According to the sculptor Gutzon Borglum, "The purpose of the memorial is to communicate the founding, expansion, preservation, and unification of the United States with colossal statues of Washington, Jefferson, Lincoln, and Theodore Roosevelt." The Mount Rushmore National Memorial experiences over three million visitors from across the globe each year. The mountain that Borglum used was originally called "the six grandfathers" by the Lakota people and named for a New York lawyer Charles E. Rushmore. Borglum and 400 workers worked for 14 years sculpturing the faces from 1927 to 1941. It was in 1933 that the National Park Service took jurisdiction of Mt. Rushmore and as each face was finished it was dedicated. Washington was dedicated in 1934 and the final of Roosevelt in 1939. In 1991, President George W. Bush officially designated Mount Rushmore.

CANDY CANE BROWNIES
www.jeffersonhotel.com

2 sticks unsalted butter
6 ounces bittersweet chocolate
2 cups granulated sugar
4 large eggs
1½ cups unbleached all-purpose flour
1 teaspoon fine sea salt
2 teaspoons pure vanilla extract
3 candy canes, finely crushed
2 York® peppermint patties, chopped

1. Preheat the oven to 350 degrees and grease a 13 x 9-inch pan.
2. In the microwave, melt butter and chocolate, stirring every 30 seconds until melted. Let the chocolate cool to room temperature.
3. In a medium bowl combine the sugar, eggs, flour, salt, and vanilla; add mixture to the cooled chocolate. Stir until completely combined. Pour the brownie batter into the prepared pan and sprinkle the crushed candy canes and chopped peppermint patties on top.
4. Bake for 25 minutes. Let cool completely before cutting into squares.

Makes 2 dozen brownies

BAILEYS IRISH CREAM CHEESE SWIRL BROWNIES

For the swirl:
3 ounces cream cheese, room temperature
2 tablespoons unsalted butter, room temperature
¼ cup sugar
1 large egg
1 tablespoon all-purpose flour
2 tablespoons Baileys Irish cream

For the brownies:
6 ounces sweet baking chocolate (I used semisweet), chopped
3 tablespoons unsalted butter, room temperature
½ cup granulated sugar
2 large eggs
½ cup all-purpose flour
½ teaspoon baking powder
¼ teaspoon fine sea salt
2 teaspoons pure vanilla extract
1 cup semisweet chocolate chips

For the glaze:
4 ounces sifted powdered sugar
1 tablespoon Baileys Irish cream
milk to thin out (amount will vary)

1. Preheat oven to 350 degrees.
2. Lightly butter an 8-inch square nonstick baking pan.
3. Using an electric mixer, beat cream cheese and butter in medium bowl until light and fluffy. Gradually add sugar and beat until well blended. Beat in egg. Mix in flour, Irish Cream, and vanilla. Set mixture aside.
4. Stir baking chocolate and butter in a heavy small saucepan over low heat until smooth. Cool slightly. Using an electric mixer, beat sugar and eggs in large bowl until slightly thickened, about 2 minutes. Mix in flour, baking powder, and salt. Mix in chocolate mixture and extracts. Stir in chocolate chips.
5. Spread half of the chocolate batter (about 1¼ cups) in prepared pan. Using a rubber spatula, spread cream cheese mixture over chocolate batter. Spoon remaining chocolate batter over top of cream cheese mixture. Using the tip of a knife, gently swirl through the batter, forming marble design. Bake brownies until tester inserted into the center comes out with a few moist crumbs attached, about 30 minutes.
6. Make glaze. Combine powdered sugar and Irish cream. If too thick thin out with milk.
7. While still warm brush (using a pastry brush) glaze over brownies. Let sit for 15 minutes. Cut into squares.

Makes 16 2-inch brownies

BANANA BREAD PUDDING

1 loaf stale French bread, cubed, with crust left on
1 quart milk (whole or 2%)
3 eggs
1 cup granulated sugar
2 tablespoons pure vanilla extract
4 ripe bananas, mashed
1 cup raisins or dried cranberries
1 teaspoon freshly ground nutmeg
1 teaspoon cinnamon
splash of Myer's rum (optional)

1. Put cubed bread in a large bowl with milk, let stand for 1 hour.
2. Pre-heat oven to 325 degrees. Spray 9 X 13-inch baking dish.
3. In another bowl beat together eggs, sugar and vanilla. Stir this mixture into the bread mixture, fold in the mashed bananas, spices and raisins.
4. Pour evenly into baking dish. Place uncovered in center of oven.
5. Bake 1 hour and 10 minutes. Remove from oven and cool to room temperature. Serve with whipped cream.

Serves 6 - 8

MAPLE CRÈME BRÛLÉE

2 eggs
1 egg yolk
⅓ cup pure maple syrup
1 teaspoon pure vanilla extract
1 cup half-and-half
2 tablespoons granulated sugar

1. Preheat oven to 350 degrees.
2. Slightly beat eggs and egg yolk. Add maple syrup and vanilla. Stir in half-and-half; mix well.
3. Divide among four 6-ounce ramekins or custard cups. Place in baking dish. Pour hot water in dish until it's halfway up sides of ramekins.
4. Place baking dish in oven and bake 35 to 40 minutes, until knife inserted near center comes out clean. Remove from baking dish and cool. Cover and chill for 2 hours.
5. Place 2 tablespoons sugar in skillet. Cook over medium-high heat until sugar begins to melt. Reduce heat to low; cook until sugar is melted and golden, about 5 minutes. Drizzle over Brûlée. Serve immediately.

Serves 4

LEMON DROP COOKIES

¼ cup unsalted butter, at room temperature
½ cup plus 2 tablespoons granulated sugar
1 extra large egg
1 teaspoon pure lemon extract
grated zest of 1 lemon
1¼ cups all-purpose flour
1 teaspoon baking soda
pinch of fine sea salt
¼ cup confectioners' sugar
2 teaspoons low-fat milk
1 teaspoon lemon extract

1. Preheat oven to 375 degrees. Lightly spray 2 cookie sheets with non-stick baking spray or place parchment paper on cookie sheets.
2. In a large bowl, beat together butter, sugar, egg, lemon extract and lemon zest with an electric mixer until light and fluffy.
3. Add the flour, baking soda, and salt; mix just until the dough comes together, the dough will be slightly sticky. Drop the dough by tablespoon at least one inch apart onto prepared cookie sheets.
4. Bake 8-10 minutes until golden brown. Set aside to cool for few minutes before putting on a rack.
5. Make glaze by putting confectioner's sugar, milk and lemon extract into a small bowl; mix well and drizzle onto cookies.

Makes about 18 cookies

CHOCOLATE PRALINE TORTE

1 cup packed brown sugar
½ cup butter
¼ cup whipping cream
¾ cup coarsely chopped pecans
1 (18¼ ounce) package devil's food cake mix
1¾ cups whipping cream
¼ cup confectioners' sugar
¼ teaspoon pure vanilla extract

1. Preheat oven to 325 degrees.
2. In a saucepan, combine the first 3 ingredients. Stir over low heat until butter is melted.
3. Pour into two 9-inch round cake pans sprayed with non-stick baking spray. Sprinkle with pecans; set aside. Prepare cake according to package directions. Carefully pour batter over pecans.
4. Place in oven and bake for 35-45 minutes or until a tester comes out clean. Cool in pans for 10 minutes inverting on a wire racks to cool completely.
5. Make topping by beating cream until soft peaks form. Add the sugar and vanilla; beat until stiff. Place one cake layer pecan side up on a serving plate. Spread with ½ the topping. Top with 2nd layer and remaining topping. Store in the refrigerator.

Serves 8-10

LEMON TART WITH BERRIES

30 square shortbread cookies (like Lorna Doone)
6 tablespoons unsalted butter, melted
¼ cup confectioners' sugar
2 eggs
3 egg yolks
¾ cup granulated sugar
½ cup fresh lemon juice
1 tablespoon grated lemon rind
½ cup cold, unsalted butter – cut into pieces
½ cup heavy cream, whipped
fresh berries (raspberries, blackberries, strawberries, blueberries, or a combination)
mint springs

1. Whirl cookies in food processor until finely crumbled. Add butter and sugar and process until combined. Spread crumbs, pressing evenly, onto bottom and sides of a 9-inch tart pan with removable bottom. Refrigerate until firm.
2. Stir eggs, egg yolks, sugar, and lemon juice together in a heavy saucepan.
3. Cook over low heat, stirring constantly until thickened and just starting to simmer (about 6-10 minutes). Do not stir too vigorously.
4. Place pan in large bowl of cold water and stir in butter until blended. Cover with waxed paper and let cool for 45 minutes. Pour filling into chilled tart shell and refrigerate to thoroughly chill.
5. Spoon or pipe whipped cream on top of tart and arrange berries on top. Garnish with mint springs if desired.

Makes 12 servings

AMERICA'S SPA

The smallest national park is Hot Springs National Park in Arkansas and comprises 5,500 acres. It has 47 thermal springs with the natural temperature being 143 degrees. The park was the first federally protected piece of land in 1832 but was not named a national park until 1921. The natural springs have been used for over 8,000 years by indigenous peoples. For more than 200 years the springs have been used to treat rheumatism and other ailments. Originally it was called Hot Springs Reservation, but soon earned the nickname "America's Spa."

KEY LIME COOKIES

½ cup butter
1 cup granulated sugar
1 egg
1 egg yolk
1½ cup unbleached all-purpose flour
1 teaspoon baking powder
½ teaspoon fine sea salt
¼ cup fresh key lime juice
1½ teaspoon grated lime peels
½ cup confectioners' sugar

1. Preheat oven to 350 degrees.
2. In a large bowl, mix butter, sugar, egg, egg yolk and lime peel until creamy.
3. In a separate bowl combine flour, baking powder, and sea salt.
4. Thoroughly mix dry ingredients with butter mixture adding lime juice.
5. Spray cookie sheet with nonstick baking spray. Form dough into ½-inch balls. Place on prepared cookie sheet.
6. Bake until lightly browned, 8 to 10 minutes. Remove to wire rack. While still warm, sift confectioners' sugar over cookies.

Makes about 3 dozen cookies

OATMEAL SPICE COOKIES

1½ cups unbleached all-purpose flour
½ teaspoon baking soda
½ teaspoon fine sea salt
2 teaspoons ground cinnamon
2 teaspoons ground cloves
2 teaspoons ground allspice
1 teaspoon ground ginger
1 cup butter, softened
1 cup granulated sugar
1 cup firmly packed brown sugar
2 eggs
1 teaspoon pure vanilla extract
3 cups oats, uncooked

1. Preheat oven to 375 degrees.
2. In a medium bowl, combine flour, baking soda, salt and spices; set aside.
3. Combine butter and sugar; cream well.
4. Beat in eggs and vanilla. Add flour mixture, mixing well. Stir in oats.
5. Drop dough on cookie sheet and bake 12 to 14 minutes or until lightly browned. Cool slightly on cookie sheet. Remove to wire racks to cool completely.

Makes 24

Mrs. Rowe's Favorite Recipes, Stanton, VA

REMEMBERING THE FALLEN

The federal Government decided that 25 battle sites deserved to be preserved because of their historical significance. The four designations include National Military Park such as Chickamauga and Chattanooga National Military Park; National Battlefield such as Antietam National Battlefield; National Battlefield Park such as Gettysburg National Battlefield Park and National Battlefield Site such Brices Cross Roads National Battlefield Site. In total there are 11 National Battlefields, nine National Military Parks, four National Battlefield Parks and one National Battlefield Site. In 1890, Chickamauga and Chattanooga National Military Park was the first such site created by Congress. These sites were originally maintained by the War Department (now Defense Department) but were transferred to the National Park Service on August 10, 1033.

ROSE KENNEDY'S SUGAR COOKIES

½ cup unsweetened butter
¼ cup granulated sugar
3 egg yolks
½ teaspoon pure vanilla extract
1 tablespoon milk
1¼ cups unbleached all-purpose flour
¼ teaspoon fine sea salt
¼ teaspoon baking powder

1. Preheat oven to 375 degrees.
2. Cream butter until light and gradually add sugar.
3. Add egg yolks, vanilla and milk; beat thoroughly.
4. Sift dry ingredients and add to batter in batches. Mix well, but do not overmix.
5. Place on unbuttered cookie sheets by teaspoons. Press down using fingers. If desired, sprinkle top with color sprinkles.
6. Bake in oven for about 8 to 10 minutes, until edges are golden.

Makes about 24

Taste and Tales of Massachusetts

PRESIDENT JOHN F. KENNEDY'S LEMON BUTTER COOKIES

1 cup butter
½ cup light brown sugar
½ cup granulated sugar
1 egg, beaten
2 tablespoons lemon juice
1 tablespoon lemon rind, grated
3 cups flour
¼ teaspoon baking soda
¼ teaspoon fine sea salt
½ cup nuts, chopped

1. Preheat oven to 400 degrees.
2. In a medium bowl, combine flour, baking soda, and sea salt.
3. In a large bowl cream butter. Add sugars and blend; add beaten egg, lemon juice and rind and mix well.
4. Gradually add dry ingredients to butter mixture until well combined. Stir in nuts.
5. Form into a roll about 2-inches in diameter, wrap in wax paper and chill in refrigerator until ready for use.
6. Slice and bake on ungreased cookie sheets for 10 to 12 minutes until golden brown around edges.

Makes 4 dozen

MASSACHUSETTS' FIRST ELECTED PRESIDENT

John Adams, the second president of the United States, was born in Quincy on October 30, 1735. In 1797, he became president and was the first president to live in the White House. In 1800, he lost his reelection campaign to Thomas Jefferson. After his defeat, he returned home to Quincy where he continued his many interests. Over the years, Adams' relationship with Jefferson was strained, but the men did communicate. On July 4, 1826, he whispered his last words to his wife and family, "Thomas Jefferson survives", not knowing that Jefferson had passed away at Monticello a few hours earlier.

Today, engraved in the fireplace in the State Dining Room at the White House is a quote from a letter written by Adams to his wife, Abigail, "I pray Heaven to bestow the best of blessings on this house and all that shall hereafter inhabit it. May none but honest and wise men ever rule under this roof."

AMERICA'S MOST FAMOUS INVENTOR

www.nps.gov/edis

Who hasn't heard of Thomas Edison? So many items used today came to us from Thomas Edison also known as the "Wizard of Menlo Park." His first invention was the phonograph which most people today have never used. Edison claimed the invention of the incandescent lightbulb which has been replaced by the LED lightbulbs. However, the lightbulb was actually invented by two other gentlemen who won a patent lawsuit against him. In his 60 years as an inventor, he acquired 1,093 patents (singly or jointly). His inventions influenced the fields of electric power generation, sound recording, motion pictures, and mass communication. Besides the historical site in New Jersey, Edison had a home on the banks of the Caloosahatchee River in Ft. Myers, Fl. which includes a museum and his workrooms (www.edisonfordwinterestates.org).

BLUEBERRY PIE

1½ cups all-purpose flour
1 stick unsalted butter, cut into small pieces
4 tablespoons ice-cold water
½ teaspoon fine sea salt or
1 box ready-made pie crust
4 cups frozen blueberries
¾ cup granulated sugar
1½ teaspoons fine sea salt
3 tablespoons cornstarch
1 tablespoon butter

1. Preheat oven to 375 degrees.
2. In a medium-sized mixing bowl, combine flour and salt. Add butter and use a pastry cutter or fingers until the mixture becomes coarse and pea-sized. Add the ice water and mix with your hands so that the dough comes together.
3. Roll the dough out into a thin, flat circle. Drape over a pie pan, trimming and shaping the edges as necessary. Cover with a plastic wrap and transfer to a refrigerator for 30 minutes.
4. In a large mixing bowl, combine blueberries, sugar, salt, and cornstarch, mixing until the blueberries are evenly coated.
5. Remove the pie crust from the refrigerator; place in pie plate and add blueberry mixture. Dot the remaining butter on top of the pie. Place second pastry on top and prick with fork.

6. Place on a pie tray in oven and cook for 60-70 minutes, until the crust has turned golden and the filling is thick and bubbling. Remove and let it cool for 1-2 hours until the filling has set. Or just eat it right away and enjoy the delicious mess.

Serves 8

Source: National Parks Foundation

COCONUT CREAM PIE

1 baked 9-inch pie shell
2 cups milk, divided
⅔ cup granulated sugar
½ teaspoon fine sea salt
3 tablespoons cornstarch
2 eggs, separated
1½ tablespoons butter
1 teaspoon pure vanilla extract
1¼ cups shredded coconut, divided
pinch of cream of tartar
2 egg whites
4 tablespoons granulated sugar

1. Preheat oven to 350 degrees.
2. Scald 1½ cups milk in top of a double boiler. Combine the ⅔ cup sugar, salt and cornstarch with remaining ½ cup milk, mixing into a smooth paste. Add to the hot milk and cook stirring until thickened.
3. In a small bowl, beat the egg yolks, add a small amount of the hot milk mixture and cook on low heat for 2 minutes. Remove from heat and mix in the butter, vanilla and ¾ cup of the coconut. Cool and pour into the pie shell.
4. Make meringue by beating the egg whites with the cream of tartar until they hold soft peaks. Gradually beat in the 4 tablespoons of sugar until it is stiff and glossy.
5. Cover the pie filling with meringue, making sure you spread meringue to cover and touch the edges of the pie shell. Sprinkle the remaining ½ cup of coconut over the meringue.
6. Bake for 5 minutes or until meringue is a delicate golden color.

Serves 6-8

Betty Groff Cookbook (2001)

THE POWER OF WATER

www.nps.gov/auca

The Canal is located in Augusta, Georgia. The Canal was built in 1845 as a source of power, water and transportation, is the only intact industrial canal in the American South in continuous use. Spearheaded by Augusta native Henry H. Cumming, who perceived that Augusta could one day become "the Lowell of the South," the Augusta Canal began to fulfill Cumming's vision in short order. By 1847 the first factories — a saw and grist mill and the Augusta Factory-were built, the first of many that would eventually line the Canal. The Canal played a role in the Civil War. The Confederate States Powder Works was the only buildings ever constructed by the government of the Confederate States of America. The 28 Powder Works structures reached along the Canal for two miles. Augusta was not ravaged by the War and was in better conditions than other Southern cities. Augusta is also home to the Masters Golf Tournament.

BANANA CREAM PIE

1 baked 9-inch pie shell
2 cups milk, divided
⅔ cup granulated sugar
½ teaspoon fine sea salt
3 tablespoons cornstarch
3 large eggs, separated
1½ tablespoons butter
1 teaspoon pure vanilla extract
1½ cups sliced bananas
1 tablespoon fresh lemon juice
pinch of cream of tartar
2 egg whites
4 tablespoons granulated sugar

1. Scald 1½ cups milk in top of a double boiler over simmering but not boiling water. Combine the sugar, salt and cornstarch with remaining ½ cup milk and stir until dissolved. Add to the hot milk and bring to a boil over boiling water; lower heat to medium and cook until thickened.
2. In a small bowl, beat the egg yolks lightly with a fork; then add several tablespoons of milk mixture and beat into yolks until well blended.
3. Add eggs to milk mixture and cook together over medium heat for 2 minutes. Remove from heat and mix in the butter and vanilla. Toss sliced bananas with lemon juice to keep them from getting brown. Spread thin layer of filling in bottom

of pie shell, then sliced bananas. Top with rest of filling and let cool while making meringue.

4. Make meringue by beating the egg whites with the cream of tartar until they hold soft peaks. Gradually beat in the 4 tablespoons of sugar until it is stiff and glossy.
5. Cover pie filling with meringue and slip under a preheated boiler until golden. Let cook and enjoy!

Serves 6-8

Cook's Note: Troyer's Dutch Heritage Restaurant in Sarasota, Florida makes the best pies, but they use a thick layer of whipped cream on top of their pies.

ORGAN OF MUSKETS

This is the Arsenal. From floor to ceiling,
Like a huge organ, rise the burnished arms;
But from their silent pipes no anthem pealing
Startles the villages with strange alarms.
Henry Wadsworth Longfellow

In 1777, the Arsenal at Springfield was established to manufacture weapons for the American Revolution.

The armory is famous for its Springfield Rifle and the M1 rifle. After two centuries of providing America's military with the finest weapons, the armory was closed in 1968.

LOW COUNTRY PEACHES AND CREAM PIE

www.bestamericanfood.net

2 pounds fresh peaches
1 standard pie shell
½ cup flour
½ cup light brown sugar
¼ teaspoon fine sea salt
1 stick butter
½ cup sugar
½ teaspoon cinnamon
1 egg
2 tablespoons heavy cream
1 teaspoon pure vanilla extract

1. Wash and peel peaches; slice thinly. Set aside. Make sure pie shell is completely thawed.
2. Mix together flour, brown sugar, and salt. Use a pastry cutter or fork to blend in butter. Mixture should resemble coarse crumbs.
3. Measure half of the flour mixture and sprinkle evenly over pie crust bottom. Place the peaches over the flour mixture. Sprinkle sugar and cinnamon over peaches.
4. Whisk together egg, cream, and vanilla and pour over sliced peaches. Top with remaining flour mixture.
5. Bake at 400 degrees for about 45 minutes.

LONGEST CAVE IN THE WORLD

www.nps.gov/maca

Mammoth Cave in Kentucky got its name from the large passages connecting to the Rotunda inside the main entrance. Humans have had access to the caves for over 6,000 years. The first Europeans to discover the cave was either John Houchin or his brother Francis in 1797. They found the large entrance to the cave while pursuing a wounded bear. The caves were owned by many different entities through the decade. It was in 1926 that some of the wealthier citizens of Kentucky formed the Mammoth Cave National Park Association and pushed to have it authorized as a national park which happened in May, 1926. Some land was acquired through donated funds and other through eminent domain. The cave is over 400 miles long making it the longest cave in the World. Today over two million people go to the Park annually while about 500,000 actually take a tour of the caves.

KENTUCKY DERBY CHOCOLATE WALNUT PIE

½ cup all-purpose flour
1 cup granulated sugar
2 eggs (lightly beaten)
½ cup butter, melted
2 tablespoons Kentucky bourbon
1 cup walnuts (chopped)
1¼ cups semisweet chocolate chips
1 teaspoon pure vanilla extract
pinch fine sea salt
1 ready-made pie crust (for 9-inch pie)

1. Preheat oven to 400 degrees.
2. Place ready-made pie crust in a 9-inch pie plate. Line the shell with wax paper and fill with rice, or beans, or pie chain. Bake shell for 15 minutes or until golden. Remove from oven and cool.
3. Reduce heat of oven to 350 degrees.
4. Combine the flour and sugar in a mixing bowl.
5. Add the eggs and butter and mix to combine. Stir in the bourbon, walnuts, chocolate chips, vanilla, and salt.
6. Pour the mixture into the baked pie crust.
7. Bake for 40 to 45 minutes, or until the filling is set. Set the pie on a wire rack and let cool before slicing.
8. Serve with whipped cream or ice cream and enjoy.

Serves 6 - 8   *Adopted from Gourmet (1974)*

FRIED PIES

It is believed that fried pies originated in Alabama.

2 cups unbleached all-purpose flour
4 tablespoons cold salted butter
½ cup cold water
2 large apples, Granny Smith and a Honeycrisp, peeled, cored, and diced
¼ cup brown sugar
½ teaspoon cinnamon
2 teaspoons Vermont boiled apple cider
1 teaspoon arrowroot
½ cup confectioners' sugar
vegetable or canola oil

1. Cut the cold butter into cubes. Add flour and using a pastry cutter, cut in the butter until it resembles coarse crumbles. Add the cold water 1 tablespoon at a time and mix with fork. When the flour mixture is moistened, gather it into a ball, wrap it in plastic and refrigerate for 30 minutes.
2. To make the filling, combine apples, brown sugar and cinnamon in a non-reactive small sauce pan. Cook on medium heat about 3 minutes or until juices start to form. Whisk the boiled apple cider and cornstarch together. Stir the mixture into the apple mixture. Turn the heat up to high and cook, stirring constantly, until mixture is thickened, about 3 minutes longer. Remove from heat and set aside.
3. Transfer the dough to a lightly floured surface. Roll the dough out to ⅛-inch thick and cut rounds with a 4-inch cookie cutter.
4. Place a heaping tablespoon apple mixture in center of each round. Moisten edges with cold water, fold in half and press edges together with a fork in order to seal.
5. Heat oil in either a deep-fryer or deep saucepan to about 350 degrees. Fry the pies, a few at a time, for 2 to 3 minutes on each side. Cook until crust is golden brown. Place on paper towels to dry. Sprinkle the top with confectioners sugar.

Makes 6 to 8

Cook's Note: I prefer to bake the pies. Preheat the oven to 350 degrees. Spray a cookie sheet with baking spray; place apple pies on sheet and bake until crust is golden brown. If you are short on time you can also cheat and use either Pillsbury crust or Grand biscuits.

SMITH ISLAND 10 LAYER CAKE

The Smith Island Cake is the official State Dessert of Maryland. Smith Island is in the Cheaspeake Bay and well worth a visit.

2 sticks unsalted butter, at room temperature, cut into chunks
2 cups granulated sugar
5 large eggs
3 cups all-purpose flour
¼ teaspoon fine sea salt
1 heaping teaspoon baking powder
1 cup evaporated milk
2 teaspoons pure vanilla extract
½ cup water
2 cups sugar
1 cup evaporated milk
5 ounces unsweetened chocolate, chopped
1 stick unsalted butter
½ to 1 teaspoon pure vanilla extract

1. Position oven rack in the middle of the oven; preheat oven to 350 degrees. Use butter to lightly grease two or three 9-inch cake pans and re-grease them as needed.
2. Cream together sugar and butter. Add eggs one at a time and beat until smooth. Sift together the flour, salt and baking powder. Mix into egg mixture one cup at a time.
3. With mixture running, slowly pour in the evaporated milk, then the vanilla and water. Mix just until uniform.
4. Put three serving spoons full of batter in each of 9-inch lightly greased pans, using the back of the spoon to spread evenly.
5. Bake three layers at a time on the middle rack of the oven for 8 minutes. A layer is done when you hold it near your ear and you do not hear it sizzle.
6. Begin making icing when the first cake pans go into the oven. Put the sugar and evaporated milk in a medium pan. Cook and stir over medium-low hear until warm. Add chocolate and cook to melt. Add butter and melt. Cook over medium heat at a slow boil for 10 to 15 minutes. Stir occasionally. Add vanilla. Icing will be thin but thickens as it cools.
7. Put the cake together as the layers are finished. Let the layers cool a bit in the pans. Run a spatula around the edge of the pan and ease the layer out of the pan. Do not worry if it tears; no one will notice when the cake is finished. Use two or three spoonfuls of icing between each layer. Cover the top and sides of the cake with the rest of the icing. Push icing that runs onto the plate back onto the cake.

Mrs. Kitching's Smith Island Cookbook (1981)

BLUEBERRY SWIRL CHEESECAKE

1½ cups blueberries
¼ cup granulated sugar
2 teaspoons cornstarch
1 tablespoon lemon juice
1 cup graham cracker crumbs
2 tablespoons granulated sugar
2 tablespoons butter, melted
1 (8 ounce) package cream cheese
1 cup granulated sugar
8 ounces sour cream
2 teaspoons pure vanilla extract
4 large eggs
2 tablespoons unbleached all-purpose flour

1. To make blueberry purée combine berries, sugar and cornstarch in a saucepan. Bring to boil over medium heat and cook, stirring 5 minutes. Puree in blender with lemon juice. Cool completely.
2. Preheat oven to 350 degrees. Wrap outside of 9-inch springform pan with heavy-duty foil. Combine cracker crumbs, sugar and butter in bowl; mix well. Press evenly into prepared pan and bake 10 minutes. Cool.
3. Beat cream cheese in mixing bowl until light and fluffy. Gradually add sugar and beat until completely smooth. Beat in sour cream and vanilla. At low speed, beat in eggs one at a time, then flour just until blended. Pour batter over crust.
4. Place pan in larger baking pan. Carefully drizzle blueberry puree over batter. Swirl knife through batter to marbleize. Place on oven rack. Pour boiling water into larger pan 1-inch up side of springform pan. Bake 1¼ hours or until just set. Turn oven off; let stand in oven 1 hour. Remove pan from water bath. Remove foil; cool completely. Cover and refrigerate overnight. Remove sides of pan.

Serves 12

NATIONAL HERITAGE AREAS

According the U.S. Department of the Interior, a "National Heritage Area is a place where natural, cultural, historic and recreational resources combine to form a cohesive, nationally-distinctive landscape arising from patterns of human activity shaped by geography. These areas tell nationally important stories about our nation and are representative of the national experience through both the physical features that remain and the traditions that have evolved within them."

NATIONAL PARKS AND THE REVOLUTIONARY WAR

www.nps.gov/mima and www.nps.gov/sara

It has been said that the Revolutionary War began in Massachusetts with the "shot heard around the world" and ended with New York. There are several national parks in Massachusetts from Fanueil Hall in Boston, to Minute Man National Historic Park that transverses Concord and Lexington. Visitors can learn all about Paul Revere's ride and the first encounter with the British. In Springfield, Mass visitors learn about the first federal armory, the Springfield Armory which houses the famous "Organ of Muskets." As the war moved west the Hudson River played a major role in who won the war. He who controlled the Hudson would win the war. General Burgoyne had march south from Canada with about 7,500 British and German soldiers and initially won battles at Ft. Ticonderoga and Ft. Anne. Things were looking good for the British until they met up with General Horatio Gates and an army of 8,000 at Saratoga. After a battle lasting several days the British retreated to the Great Redoubt on the Hudson River. There they surrendered to the vastly superior American forces. The British marched out of camp "with the Honors of War" and surrendered their arms along the Hudson River's West bank.

HUMMINGBIRD CAKE

3 cups all-purpose flour, plus more for pans
2 cups granulated sugar
1 teaspoon fine sea salt
1 teaspoon baking soda
1 teaspoon ground cinnamon
3 large eggs, beaten
1½ cups vegetable oil
1½ teaspoons pure vanilla extract
1 (8 ounce) can crushed pineapple in juice, undrained
2 cups chopped ripe bananas (about 6 bananas)
1 cup chopped pecans, toasted
vegetable shortening

Frosting

2 (8 ounce) packages cream cheese, softened
1 cup salted butter, softened
2 (16 ounce) packages powdered sugar
2 teaspoons pure vanilla extract
¾ cup pecan halves, toasted

1. Prepare the cake layers: Preheat oven to 350 degrees. Whisk together flour, sugar, salt, baking soda and cinnamon in a large bowl; add eggs and oil, stirring just until dry ingredients are moistened. Stir in vanilla, pineapple, bananas, and toasted pecans.

2. Spray three 9-inch round cake pans with baking spray. Divide batter evenly among the three pans.
3. Bake in preheated oven until a wooden pick inserted in center comes out clean, 25 to 30 minutes. Cool in pans on wire racks 10 minutes. Remove from pans to wire racks, and cool completely, about 1 hour.
4. Prepare the cream cheese frosting: Beat cream cheese and butter with an electric mixer on medium-low speed until smooth. Gradually add powdered sugar, beating at low speed until blended after each addition. Stir in vanilla. Increase speed to medium-high, and beat until fluffly, 1 to 2 minutes.
5. Assemble cake: Place 1 cake layer on a serving platter; spread top with 1 cup of the frosting. Top with second layer and spread with 1 cup frosting. Top with third layer, and spread remaining frosting over top and sides of cake. Arrange pecan halves on top of cake.
6. Prepare cupcakes instead: Place 24 paper baking cups in 2 (12-cup) standard-size muffin pans. Spoon batter into prepared cups, filling about three-quarters full. Bake at 350 degrees until a wooden pick inserted in center comes out clean, 18 to 20 minutes. Let cool and either pipe or spread onto cupcakes.

Cook's Note: I have been making this cake since Southern Living first published it in 1978. Over the years it has become their most requested recipe. Instead of making a layered cake, I have made it in 9 x 13-inch pans and even 2 9-inch square pans. No matter which way you make it, it is delicious!!

WIND BENEATH THEIR WINGS

www.nps.gov/wrbr

Once upon a time there were two brothers, Orville and Wilbur Wright, from Indiana who from an early age were fascinated with the prospects of flight. Their love of all things aeronautical began when their father gave them a toy helicopter in 1878. Neither of the boys went to college, but had an interest in all things mechanical. The brothers closely followed the research of German aviator Otto Lilienthal and when he died in a glider crash they began experimenting with flight. They began testing their prototypes in Kitty Hawk, North Carolina which is known for its high winds. Finally, on December 17, 1903, they flew their plane for 59 seconds at 852 feet and as they say, "the rest is history."

CRADLE OF LIBERTY

"The City of Boston, the Cradle of Liberty, may Faneuil Hall ever stand a monument to teach the world that resistance to oppression is a duty, and will, under true republican institutions become a blessing."

General Lafayette, 1825

Constructed in 1740, Faneuil Hall earned its nickname, Cradle of Liberty, because it was used as a meeting place for American patriots before and during the Revolutionary War. In 1805, American architect Charles Bulfinch designed an addition to Faneuil Hall that allowed it to hold up to 1,000 people. Today, it is the cornerstone of Quincy Market and is still in use as a museum and meeting hall.

Coconut Rice Pudding

2¾ cups water

¾ cup long-grain white rice

1 (15 ounce) can cream of coconut

1 (12 ounce) can evaporated milk

⅔ cup sweetened flaked coconut (optional)

1 tablespoon dark rum (optional)

1. In a 6-quart slow-cooker bowl, stir water, rice, cream of coconut, and evaporated milk until combined. Cover and cook on low setting 4 to 5 hours or on high setting 2½ to 3 hours.
2. Toast coconut: Heat nonstick small skillet over medium heat until hot. Add coconut; cook 4 to 5 minutes or until lightly browned, stirring constantly. Transfer coconut to plate.
3. Remove bowl from slow cooker. Stir in rum, if using. Let pudding stand 10 minutes. Transfer pudding to serving bowl. If not serving right away, press sheet of plastic wrap onto pudding; refrigerate up to 2 days.
4. To serve, spoon pudding into dessert bowls; sprinkle with toasted coconut if using.

Preserves and More

FANEUIL HALL

WINTER AT VALLEY FORGE

www.nps.gov/vafo

During the winter of 1777-78, with the British in Philadelphia, General George Washington decided to encamp at Valley Forge. His reasoning was that Valley Forge was a naturally defensible plateau where they could train and recover from the year's battles while winter weather, impassable roads, and scant supplies stopped the fighting. On December 19th, 1777, 12,000 soldiers and 400 women and children marched into Valley Forge and began to build what would become the fourth largest city in the United States, with 1,500 log huts and two miles of fortifications. Lasting six months, from December until June, the encampment was as diverse as any city, with people who were free and enslaved, wealthy and impoverished, speakers of several languages, and adherents of several religions. Another example of America's melting pot.

WARM BACON DRESSING

I originally had this dressing on wilted lettuce at the Fairfield Inn in Fairfield, PA. It was delicious. The Inn is one of the oldest in the nation having been in continuous operation since 1757.

12 slices bacon
1 tablespoon Dijon mustard
2 tablespoons balsamic vinegar
3 tablespoons honey
fine sea salt to taste
freshly ground black pepper to taste

1. In a heavy fry pan, stir and fry bacon over medium heat. When crisp, remove bacon to drain on paper plates or towels.
2. Pour off all put two tablespoons bacon fat. With a wire whisk, mix in mustard, vinegar and honey; blend until smooth. Season with salt and pepper. Pour over salad greens immediately.

CORN RELISH

6 cups Basic Pickling Syrup, using 4 cups white vinegar instead of cider vinegar and water
8 cups corn kernels, fresh or frozen
2 cups chopped cabbage
1 cup chopped onion
½ cup chopped green bell pepper
½ cup chopped red bell pepper

1. Place everything in an 8-quart kettle. Bring to boil and simmer over medium heat for 10 minutes.
2. Ladle into hot sterilized jars, filling to neck of each jar and seal with new lids and rings. Let stand for 12 hours before moving them to cool storage areas to prevent breaking seals. Refrigerate after opening.

Serves 8 pints

A UNIQUE AFRICAN AMERICAN CULTURE

The Gullah Geechee people are descendants of enslaved Africans from various ethnic groups of west and central Africa. Their ancestors were brought to the New World and forced to work on the plantations of coastal South Carolina, Georgia, North Carolina and Florida. Established in 2006, the Gullah Geechee Cultural Heritage Corridor seeks to preserve many African practices in their language, arts, crafts and cuisine. Gullah is a unique creole language spoken along the Sea Islands and adjacent coastal areas of South Carolina and Georgia. It is the only distinctly African creole language in the United States and has influenced traditional Southern vocabulary and speech patterns. Famous for their sweetgrass baskets which were originally designed for rice production and processing and other domestic uses in Africa, were used for agricultural purposes such as planting and harvesting of coastal crops. Food, as in most cultures, has always played an important role in social traditions. Gatherings, celebrations, and religious rituals, are often accompanied by food.

PATERSON'S GREAT FALLS

www.nps.gov/pagr

Alexander Hamilton, Secretary of U.S. Treasury, envisioned the economy of the United States as being industrial based. In 1791, he pulled together a variety of individuals to establish the Society for Establishing Useful Manufactures to develop factories along the Passaic River in New Jersey. The Great Falls are the second largest falls east of the Mississippi in volume and Pierre Charles L'Enfant took the waters to develop an intricate system to power the factories. Be it cotton duck for sails, the first continuous sheet paper, the first revolver by Samuel Colt, and the first practical submarine by John Holland, Paterson became the world's center for the production of cotton, silk and locomotives. All these industries earned Paterson the title of America's first planned industrialized city. In 1913, the "Silk Strike" happened when workers demanded an eight-hour day. Hamilton's visions of an industrialized nation became the basis of capitalism.

BASIC PICKLING SYRUP

4 cups granulated sugar
2 cups cider vinegar
2 cups water
1 teaspoon fine sea salt
1 tablespoon celery seed
1 tablespoon mustard seed
1 tablespoon pickling spices (optional)

1. Combine all ingredients in large saucepan, stir and bring to boil. Simmer 5 minutes over medium-high heat, adding any extra spices pickle recipe calls for.
2. Remove from heat and pour into sterilized jars. Seal with new lids if you are not using it within a day or two. Syrup will keep for several weeks in refrigerator.

Makes 6 cups

Cook's Note: Combine a variety of spices such as mustard seed, allspice berries, whole coriander seeds, whole cloves, ground ginger, crushed red pepper flakes, bay leaf, crumbled, 2-inch cinnamon stick, dill seed, and ginger; place in a cheesecloth bag.

SPICED PUMPKIN AND PECAN BUTTER

Zest of 1 orange or zest of ½ orange and ½ lemon removed in wide strips with a swivel peeler

1 (29-ounce) can solid pack pumpkin plus ½ cup of water or 3½ to 4 cups pumpkin puree prepared from scratch

2 cups light brown sugar, firmly packed

3 tablespoons strained fresh orange juice

3 tablespoons strained fresh lemon juice

1½ teaspoons ground cinnamon

½ teaspoon fine sea salt

¼ teaspoon ground allspice

¼ teaspoon ground ginger

pinch of ground cloves

⅓ cup pecans, lightly toasted and very finely chopped

1. Simmer the orange zest in 2 cups of water in a saucepan for 10 minutes, then drain it and mince it to a fine pulp. Measure out 1 tablespoon and reserve.
2. Combine in a heavy-bottomed stainless-steel or other nonreactive saucepan, the pumpkin and water (if using canned) orange zest, sugar, orange juice, lemon juice, cinnamon, salt, allspice, ginger and cloves. Bring to a boil over medium-high heat, stirring constantly; lower the heat and simmer the mixture, stirring it very often with a wooden spatula, until it has become very thick, about 15 minutes. Sample the butter and add more of the spices to taste.
3. Stir in the pecans and continue to cook for another 2 to 3 minutes. Ladle the boiling-hot pumpkin butter into clean, hot half-pint canning jars, leaving ¼-inch headspace. Seal the jars with new canning lids according to manufacturer's instructions. Process the jars for 10 minutes in a boiling water bath. Cool, label, and store for up to a year in a cool cupboard.

Makes 5 cups

REMEMBER THE RAISIN
www.nps.gov/rira

River Raisin National Battlefield Park in Michigan preserves, commemorates, and interprets the January 1813 battles of the War of 1812. The Battle resulted in the greatest victory for Tecumseh's American Indian confederation and the greatest defeat for the United States. The battle comprised soldiers from Canada, Britain, French, American, and Native Americans and was one of the bloodiest of the War of 1812. Hundreds of American soldiers died during the battle that spawned the battle cry, "Remember the Raisin!" The River Raisin National Battlefield Park was established as the 393rd unit of the United States National Park Service which was signed into law on March 30, 2009.

CALAMONDIN MARMALADE

2 quarts calamondins, washed
7 cups sugar, divided

1. Cut up calamondins and remove all seeds. Put 8 cups of fruit in blender or processor and chop fine.
2. In a large pot, put the chopped calamondins and 1 cup sugar; let stand 15 minutes.
3. Add 6 more cups sugar, stir and bring to full rolling boil for 1 minute. Turn heat down to medium, and cook 10 minutes, stirring and skimming occasionally.
4. Put in hot sterilized jars and seal or keep refrigerated.

Yields: 8 small jars

SACRED SPACE
www.nps.gov/emfo

In Harper's Ferry, Iowa along the Mississippi River are the Effigy's Mounds sacred to the Native Americans. These mounds go back to 1400-750 B.P. and are associated with the culture known today as the Effigy Moundbuilders. Mounds of earth in the shapes of birds, bear, deer, bison, lynx, turtle, panther or water spirit are the most common images. Like earlier groups, the Effigy Moundbuilders continued to build conical mounds for burial purposes. Two major shapes associated with Effigy Mounds are the bear and the bird.

BRANDIED APRICOTS

2 cups granulated sugar
¾ cup water
¼ teaspoon fine sea salt
1½ teaspoons cider vinegar
2 pounds fresh apricots
1 cup brandy

1. In a large enamel or stainless steel saucepan combine sugar, water, salt, and vinegar. Bring to boil over high heat and add apricots. Reduce heat to medium and simmer for 10 to 12 minutes, depending on size of apricots.
2. Remove fruit and let syrup boil over medium heat for 8 minutes more. Remove pan from heat, add brandy and fruit and blend together. Ladle apricots and syrup into hot sterilized jars and seal with new lids and rings.
3. Do not move jars for 12 hours to prevent seals from breaking. Store away from direct sunlight for several weeks at least before serving.

Makes 4 pints

Classic Pennsylvania Dutch Cooking (1990)

Cook's Note: Can also substitute peaches or pears.

RED ONION JAM

¼ cup pure olive oil
3 medium red onions, minced
fine sea salt
freshly ground black pepper
⅔ cup sherry wine vinegar
2 tablespoons unsalted butter
½ cup granulated sugar

1. Heat a large saucepan over medium heat. When hot, add the oil then the onions and season with salt and pepper. Toss well then allow the onions to caramelize, tossing now and then, to ensure even cooking.
2. When the onions turn translucent they begin to caramelize, deglaze with the vinegar, cooking down until all the liquid is almost gone, then add the butter and sugar and stir well. Cook, stirring occasionally, until the mixture thickens to where very little liquid remains and it begins to hiss when stirred.
3. When you have reached your desired consistency, remove the pan from the heat and transfer the jam to a clean glass jar. Alternatively, let the jam cool before transferring it to a bowl to cool completely. Refrigerate in an airtight container for up to 3 months.

Makes 2 cups

MAKO SICA
www.nps.gov/badl

This is what the Lakota called the area known as the badlands. The Badlands National Park (Lakota: Makȟóšiča) covers 242,756 acres of sharply eroded buttes and pinnacles, along with the largest undisturbed mixed grass prairie in the United States. Millions of years ago the ancient skeleton such as the ancient camels, three-toed horses, rhinos, and saber-toothed cat once roamed here. Today, bison, bighorn sheep, prairie dogs, and black-footed ferrets roam the mixed grass prairie. Nearly 65,000 acres of the Park has been designated a wilderness area. The black-footed ferrets, one of the World's most endangered mammals, were re-introduced into the Park and have been making a comeback abet a slow one. Initially, the area was authorized as Badlands National Monument on March 4, 1929. It was re-designated a national park on November 10, 1978. The movie, Dances with Wolves and Thunderheart were both filmed in the Park. The scenery looks like from another planet, but once again the wisdom to preserve these lands for future generations was the right thing to do.

WALK INTO 500 YEARS OF HISTORY

www.nps.gov/saju

San Juan was founded by the Spanish in 1521 and several years later the first fortified defenses at Castillo San Felipe del Morro and La Fortaleza were built with batteries aimed at the harbor entrance. These defenses were part of Castillo San Cristóbal that was completed in 1783. The Castillo covered 27 acres of land and was basically wrapped around the city of San Juan. Due to a growing population, about a third of the fortification was demolished in 1897 to ease traffic in and out of the walled city. On May 10, 1898, the first shot of the Spanish-American War was ordered by Captain Mendez against the USS Yale. Six months later the Treaty of Paris ended the Spanish-American War with Puerto Rico becoming a U.S. territory.

MANGO CHUTNEY

6 mangoes
1 pound dates
2 pounds brown sugar
¼ pound crystallized and or preserved ginger, chopped
1 pound seedless golden raisins or dried cranberries
¾ tablespoon fine sea salt
cayenne pepper
1 quart cider vinegar
1 teaspoon cinnamon
1 teaspoon dry mustard
1 teaspoon garlic, minced

1. Peel and slice the mangoes. Pit dates and dice.
2. Place all ingredients in a large, heavy pot; simmer until thick, about 2 to 3 hours, stirring as needed to prevent sticking.
3. Store in sterilized jars in refrigerator. It will keep indefinitely.

Yields: 6 pints

KEY LIME CURD

½ cup butter
1¼ cups sugar
½ cup Key Lime juice
1 teaspoon grated lime zest
6 egg yolks

1. Combine the butter, sugar and lime juice in a medium saucepan. Cook over medium heat until the sugar has dissolved.
2. Add the lime zest and the egg yolks, one at a time, whisking constantly. Do not allow to boil. Continue to whisk until the mixture is thick and smooth, about 15 minutes.
3. Remove from the heat and chill the curd before using.

Makes 1 cup

CRANBERRY ORANGE MARMALADE

2 oranges
1 lemon
2½ cups water
3 cups fresh cranberries
1 (1¾ ounce) package powdered fruit pectin
6½ cups sugar

1. Remove peel from oranges and lemon. Scrape out white membrane and cut peel into thin strips.
2. Add peel to 2½ cups water in large saucepan and cook, covered, over low heat 20 minutes.
3. Section oranges and lemon, discard membranes, and cut fruit into small pieces.
4. Add with cranberries to peel and simmer 10 minutes, stirring constantly. Stir in pectin and bring to a boil. Stir in sugar; bring to a full rolling boil. Boil hard 1 minute, stirring constantly.
5. Remove from heat and skim foam, if any. Let stand 15 minutes, stirring now and then.
6. Ladle into hot, clean pint jars to within ⅛-inch of top. Wipe rims and put on lids. Put on screw bands and tighten as tightly as possible by hand. Process in boiling water bath 5 minutes.

Makes 4 pints

THE BATTLE THAT SAVED MISSOURI

www.nps.gov/peri

Keeping Missouri in the Union was a prime objective of the Federal government during the first year of the Civil War. This objective was behind the two battles in Missouri – one in Wilson Creek and the other Pea Ridge. The Confederate won the first battle at Wilson Creek necessitating the battle at Pea Ridge. The Confederate leader, Maj. Gen. Earl Van Dorn, with his 16,000-man army and led it north to capture St. Louis. The Union leader, Brig. Gen. Curtis, with 10,500 troops were dug in across his path on the bluffs above Little Sugar Creek. Since attacking straight on was not a good idea, Van Dorn planned to swing around behind them and strike at dawn. As we know the best laid plans often go awry. The delay of Van Dorn allowed Curtis to face about and prepare for the attack. With the hierarchy of the Confederate troops either killed or captured, many troops scattered from the field. The next morning March 8, 1862 there was an artillery barrage that crippled the Confederate line. Van Dorn ordered his troops to withdraw. The battle of Pea Ridge was over and Missouri remained in the Union and politically neutral throughout the war.

MUSTARD BEER SAUCE

½ cup Dijon mustard

2 tablespoons light brown sugar

2 tablespoons beer

⅛ to ¼ teaspoon ground red pepper to taste

Stir together all ingredients.

Yields: ⅔ cup

KEY LIME SAUCE

2 tablespoons butter

2 tablespoons flour

1½ cups cream

fine sea salt to taste

freshly ground black pepper to taste

2 tablespoons fresh dill (or to taste)

1 cup sliced mushrooms

¼ cup white wine

juice of 2 limes (preferably Key lime)

1. Using butter and flour, make a roux. Slowly blend in the cream to a smooth consistency.
2. Add seasonings to taste, the mushrooms, wine and lime juice; heat.
3. Serve over entrees such as stuffed chicken breast.

Yields: 2 cups

RÉMOULADE SAUCE

¾ cup mayonnaise
2 teaspoons Dijon mustard
1½ teaspoons whole-grain mustard
1 teaspoon tarragon vinegar
¼ teaspoon Tabasco® sauce
2 teaspoons drained tiny capers, chopped
1 tablespoon chopped fresh flat-leaf parsley
1 thinly sliced scallion (3 inches of green left on)
fine sea salt
freshly ground black pepper, to taste

1. Combine ingredients in a bowl. Set aside, covered, in the refrigerator.

STRAWBERRY VINEGAR

1½ cups hulled and roughly chopped strawberries
1½ cups white wine vinegar
½ cup granulated sugar

1. Place strawberries and vinegar in a jar with a tight-fitting lid. Let stand in a sunny window 3 to 4 days (the vinegar will become bright red). Strain into a small saucepan and discard berries.
2. Stir in sugar and heat over medium heat until mixture comes to a boil. Simmer over low heat about 10 minutes.
3. Cool and pour into a clean bottle. Cover and store in a cool, dry place or in the refrigerator.

Makes about 2 cups.

TARRAGON VINEGAR

1 cup fresh tarragon leaves, washed and dried well
1 cup champagne vinegar

1. Bruise the tarragon leaves just slightly with the back of a wooden spoon. Just bruise slightly, do not cut.
2. Add leaves to a small mason jar or container.
3. Pour vinegar over leaves and place on lid. Let sit in a cool, dry place for at least a week, preferably longer to let the tarragon flavor develop. Give the container a shake once or twice a day.
4. Strain the tarragon leaves from the vinegar. Can put vinegar in either a fancy jar with a sprig of tarragon for visual effect.

Makes 1 cup

GINGER PEACHES

1 teaspoon fresh ginger (grated)
2 tablespoons butter
2 cups peaches sliced (fresh or canned)

1. Cook fresh grated ginger in butter. Add peach slices (fresh or canned).
2. Warm and mix.
3. Serve as a side dish with ham or chicken.

GIVE ME YOUR POOR

To celebrate our nations 100th birthday, the people of France gave the Statue of Liberty to the people of the United States. The Lady was designed by Frederic Auguste Bartholdi and is a robed female figure representing Libertas, the Roman Goddess of Freedom. She bears a torch in her right hand and holds a tableau in her left. The date of the American Revolution, July 4, 1776, is inscribed on the tableau. During the early part of the 1900s, generations of immigrants passed by the statue on their way to Ellis Island. On the pedestal the following words are inscribed:

"Give me your tired, your poor,
Your huddled masses yearning to breathe free,
The wretched refuse of your teeming shore.
Send these, the homeless, tempest-tossed to me,
I lift my lamp beside the golden door!"

CINNAMON HOT APPLE SAUCE

2 tablespoons unsalted butter
½ cup granulated sugar
2 tablespoons grenadine syrup
2 cups sliced tart apples
2 tablespoons sour cream
2 tablespoons heavy cream
¾ teaspoon cornstarch
1 tablespoon apple brandy (optional

1. Melt the butter in a medium skillet over moderate heat. Add the sugar, syrup and apple slices. Stir to coat the slices. Cover and cook, stirring once, until the apples are translucent, about 5 minutes.
2. Stir together the sour cream, heavy cream and cornstarch. Stir the mixture into the apples. Bring to a boil, cook for 1 minute and remove from heat. Stir in the apple brandy.

Makes 1½ cups

Vegetables

STATUE OF LIBERTY

BATTLE OF FALLEN TIMBERS

www.nps.gov/fati

This Battle resulted in the dispossession of American Indian tribes and a loss of colonial territory for the British military and settlers in the Old Northwest Territory. The entire Battle took only three days and at the end the American militiamen under the command of Major General Anthony Wayne had defeated over 1,000 Indians warriors from Ohio and the Great Lakes tribes. In 1795, they signed the Treaty of Greenville which gave control of the region and river crossings to the United States giving them domination over the Indian tribes. The Jay Treaty of 1796 formally ended British presence in the Old Northwest Territory. It was not until the War of 1812 which finally settle the boundary and disputes of Lake Erie which was British naval power.

SUMMER VEGETABLE RICOTTA TART

1 prepared pie crust
2 large eggs, lightly beaten
1 generous cup of part skim ricotta cheese
4 tablespoons half and half
½ cup Parmesan cheese
pinch of your favorite fresh herbs
fine sea salt to taste
freshly ground black pepper to taste
2 cups sautéed mixed veggies of choice, diced
2 tomatoes, sliced thin
grated Swiss Cheese

1. Preheat oven 350 degrees.
2. Place pie crust in a deep pie plate.
3. Sauté vegetables for 10 minutes starting with more denser vegetables such as potatoes.
4. In a mixing bowl combine ricotta cheese, eggs, milk, Parmesan cheese, herbs, salt, pepper and the veggies once done.
5. Pour into prepared pie crust and top with sliced tomato and grated cheese. Bake for 40 to 45 minutes.

Serves 6 - 8

Cook's Note: Serve as an appetizer, side dish or a light lunch. Delicious with a white wine, Sangria or lemonade.

TOMATO-ZUCCHINI TART

½ (15 ounce) package refrigerated piecrusts
1 medium zucchini, thinly sliced (about ¾ pound)
2 teaspoons olive oil
3 medium plum tomatoes, sliced
½ cup fresh basil, chopped
⅓ cup (1½ ounce) freshly grated Parmesan cheese
⅓ cup light mayonnaise
½ teaspoon freshly ground pepper

1. Preheat oven to 450 degrees.
2. Place piecrust into a 9-inch tart pan according to package directions; trim excess. Prick bottom and sides of piecrust using a fork. Place pie weights or peas in bottom before baking.
3. Bake piecrust for 9 to 11 minutes or until lightly browned. Let cool. Remove weights. Lower temperature of oven to 425 degrees.
4. Sauté zucchini in hot oil in a large skillet over medium-high heat 2 minutes or until tender. Arrange zucchini in bottom of prepared piecrust. Arrange tomatoes on top of zucchini.
5. Stir together basil, cheese, and mayonnaise. Drop by teaspoonfuls evenly on top of tomatoes and spread gently. Sprinkle with pepper.
6. Bake at 425 degrees for 10 to 15 minutes or until thoroughly heated and cheese mixture is slightly melted.

Serves 8

BABY ZUCCHINI WITH GARLIC POTATOES

2 tablespoons extra virgin olive oil
2 medium Russet potatoes, washed, sliced ¼-inch thick
2 garlic cloves, chopped
½ pound baby zucchini, sliced ½-inch thick
1 tablespoon fresh thyme, chopped
fine sea salt to taste
freshly ground black pepper to taste

1. Prepare a large non-stick sauté pan coated with 2 tablespoons oil over medium-high heat.
2. Sauté the potatoes until browned on both sides, about 2 minutes. Add the baby zucchini, chopped garlic and thyme.
3. Season with sea salt and pepper, cover, and cook mixture until potatoes are fork tender, about 10 minutes.

Serves 4

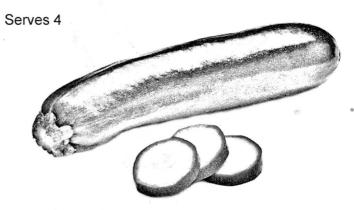

WATERWAY TO THE INTERIOR
www.nps.gov/erie

The canal connected the Great Lakes to New York's Hudson River and Lake Champlain and was called both "Clinton's Big Ditch" and "the ditch that salt built" since salt tax revenues paid for half the cost of construction of the canal. It was longer by far, 363 miles in length, than any other canal previously built in Europe or America. It has been expanded and enlarged twice with the latest being the Barge Canal which was completed in 1918. At the time of construction 32 aqueducts and 83 locks were built on the canal. Besides the Erie Canal, there were several feeder canals that made up the system. One from Lake Erie to the Finger Lakes, another north to Lake Ontario and the third from Troy, New York to Lake Champlain. One connected the south end of Seneca Lake to Elmira and was an important route for Pennsylvania coal and timber into the canal system. Today most travel on the canal systems is for recreational purposes, but over the past few years there has been a growth in the amount of commercial traffic. For those who want to experience travel as our forefathers, contact the Erie Canal Cruise Company (www.eriecanal-cruise.com).

FRIED GREEN TOMATOES

2 firm green tomatoes, sliced ¼ to ½ -inch thick
1 cup corn meal
fine sea salt to taste
dash sugar
cooking oil (or bacon drippings)

1. Mix corn meal, salt and sugar. Dip tomato slices into corn meal.
2. Fry tomatoes in oil until brown, turning once. Remove from oil and drain on paper towels. Serve hot.

Serves 4

FREE LAND WAS THE CRY!
www.nps.gov/home

In 1862, the Homestead Act enticed millions to head west with the promise of free land. Carl Sandburg said that the Homestead Act provided "a farm free to any man who wanted to put a plow into unbroken sod." The Act encouraged migration Westward providing settlers 160 acres of public land. Approximately four million claims were made with about 270 million acres of land distributed by the Act.

LATKES

1 large potato
2 large zucchinis
fine sea salt
1 bunch scallions
2 eggs, beaten
½ cup whole wheat flour
freshly ground black pepper
4 tablespoons canola or olive oil
1 cup lowfat sour cream
1 bunch chives

1. Clean and scrub, but do not peel, the potato and zucchini. Using a box grater, grate potato and zucchini into a colander and toss with a teaspoon of fine sea salt. Let sit for about 10 minutes, then scoop up about a handful into a clean dish cloth. Wring out over the sink. Place dried grated vegetables into a large bowl. Repeat, switching to a clean dry dish towel if need be, until you've dried all the grated vegetables. You want the potato and zucchini to be very dry at this point.
2. Slice the scallions into ¼-inch slices and add to grated veggies in bowl. Add the flour, beaten eggs, and pepper to taste and stir to combine. Add in a few extra dashes of salt if you like.
3. Chop chives and combine with sour cream in a separate bowl.
4. Heat 1 tablespoon of oil in non-stick skillet over medium heat. Pick up about a handful of veggie mixture, and shape into a ball in your palm. Smoosh it into a cake by flattening it with your other hand and add to skillet.
5. Repeat until you fill the pan, making sure not to crowd your pancakes. Cook about 3 minutes, until the bottoms are golden, and the cakes have set, being careful not to burn the bottoms. Then flip cakes over and continue cooking approximately another 2 to 3 minutes. Remove to a plate lined with a paper towel. Adding more oil to the pan as needed, repeat until all the pancakes are cooked. If not serving immediately, these keep very well in a warm oven. Serve topped with dollops of sour cream and chives.

Serves 6

WILD RICE WITH APPLE

1½ cups water
½ cup orange juice
3 tablespoons lime juice
2 cups wild rice, cooked
2 cups long grain rice, cooked
1 cup apple, peeled and chopped
1 cup frozen green peas, thawed

1. Combine water, orange and lime juice in medium saucepan. Bring to a boil. Pour in long grain and the wild rice. Stir rice once, cover and reduce heat to simmer. Cook for 30 minutes or until liquid is totally absorbed.
2. Mix cooked rice with apple and green peas. Serve hot with chicken or pork.

Serves 6

Cook's Note: The secret to good rice is to stir it only once. After all moisture is absorbed you may stir it again.

WARM POTATO SALAD WITH BACON AND SHALLOTS

½ pound sliced bacon
8 shallots, sliced
½ cup chicken stock
4 tablespoons white wine vinegar
12-15 small new potatoes, boiled in their skins and still warm
fine sea salt
freshly ground pepper

1. Cut the bacon crosswise into ½-inch strips and fry in a frying pan large enough to hold the potatoes. When the bacon is almost crisp, add the shallots and cook for another minute or two.
2. Add the stock and vinegar and stir well. Slice the warm potatoes into the pan, season with salt and pepper, and gently but thoroughly mix everything together until well combined and the potatoes have absorbed most of the liquid.
3. Transfer to a salad bowl and serve at once, while still warm.

Serves 6

APPLES AND BUTTERNUT SQUASH

1 large butternut squash, peeled and cubed
2 large Granny Smith apples, cored and slice
½ cup fresh cranberries, halved
½ cup brown sugar
¼ cup butter, melted
1 tablespoon flour
1 teaspoon fine sea salt
½ teaspoon mace

1. Preheat oven to 350 degrees.
2. Place peeled and cubed squash into ungreased baking dish. Arrange apple slices on top; sprinkle with cranberries.
3. Combine remaining ingredients in a small bowl. Sprinkle mixture over squash and apples. Cover with foil.
4. Bake 50-60 minutes or until squash is tender.

Serves 6

DAWN OF THE ATOMIC AGE
www.nps.gov/mapr

Most of us think that the Atomic Bomb was developed in New Mexico when in fact a good deal of the administrative and military headquarters for the 75,000 individuals who built the industrial complex is in the East End of Oak Ridge, Tennessee. The Manhattan Project was approved by President Franklin D. Roosevelt on December 28, 1942, work on the east Tennessee site where the first production facilities were to be built was already underway. This became the site for the pilot plutonium plant and the uranium enrichment plant. The actual town of Oak Ridge was where the administrative offices were while the four plants were in the valleys away from the town. This provided security and containment in case of accidental explosions. The X-10 Graphite Reactor was a pilot plant facility based on design and engineering information developed at the Metallurgical Laboratory at the University of Chicago. After thousands of uranium slugs were loaded, the pile went critical in the early morning of November 4, 1943 and produced its first plutonium by the end of the month. The rest is history!

ASPARAGUS WITH HONEY MUSTARD DRESSING

2 bunches asparagus, peeled and trimmed
1 teaspoon lemon zest
½ cup low fat yogurt
1 tablespoon Dijon mustard
1 tablespoon sherry vinegar
1 tablespoon honey
fine sea salt to taste
freshly ground pepper to taste
2 tablespoons chopped herbs (such as mint, chives, or parsley)

1. Arrange asparagus in a steamer basket over ½ - inch water in a wok or saucepan, and steam about 2 minutes or just until bright green. Rinse with cold water until completely cooled; drain and chill.
2. Combine lemon zest and next five ingredients in a small bowl and stir until smooth.
3. Add sea salt. Pepper and herbs. Chill dressing in an airtight container.
4. Serve by placing asparagus on serving dish and spoon dressing over asparagus.

Serves 4 - 6

RUM-GLAZED CARROTS

½ cup (1 stick) butter
3 pounds whole medium carrots, trimmed
½ cup packed dark brown sugar
½ cup dark rum
¼ cup dried cranberries
½ teaspoon pepper

1. Melt the butter in a large skillet over medium heat. Add the carrots and toss to coat with the butter. Cook, turning every 10 minutes, until just tender and beginning to brown, about 30 minutes.
2. Combine the brown sugar, rum, cranberries, and pepper in a bowl; mix well. Pour evenly over the carrots. Reduce the heat to low and cook for 10 minutes, stirring occasionally. Spoon into a bowl and serve hot.

Serves 8

Cook's Note: Carrots should remain whole while cooking. Use two utensils such as fork and spoon and turn the carrots gently.

CORN SOUFFLÉ

1 cup milk
4 large eggs, separated
2 tablespoons butter, soften to room temperature
1 teaspoon fine sea salt
½ teaspoon freshly ground black pepper
½ cup cornmeal
¼ cup unbleached all-purpose flour
1 cup corn kernels, fresh or frozen
1 cup grated Cheddar cheese
1 tablespoon chopped pimento
1½ teaspoons chopped fresh chives

1. Preheat oven to 375 degrees.
2. Heat milk in large, heavy saucepan over medium-high heat until very hot but not boiling. While heating milk, beat egg yolks and butter together in a large mixing bowl until fluffy.
3. Combine salt, pepper, cornmeal, and flour together in another bowl and gradually whisk into hot milk, stirring constantly until thickened.
4. Remove from heat and beat into egg yolk mixture.
5. Whip egg whites until they form soft peaks. Fold corn, cheese, pimiento, and chives into yolk mixture. Gently fold into egg whites.
6. Pour into greased baking dish and bake for 30 minutes or until golden brown and will not jiggle in middle when shaken.

Serves 4 *Classic Pennsylvania Dutch Cooking (1990)*

IRON PLANTATIONS CHANGE AMERICAN INDUSTRY
www.nps.gov/hofu

Hopewell Furnace showcases an early American industrial landscape from natural resource extraction to enlightened conservation. Operating from 1771-1883, Hopewell and other "iron plantations" laid the foundation for the transformation of the United States into an industrial giant. These "plantations" were actually small villages or company towns. Because in the beginning the site would be remote from villages or towns, the ironmaster had also to provide some housing for them, Even back in the days of the plantation, there was foreign competition and in order to keep prices competitive, the ironmaster could not pay wages adequate for his employees to purchase their food, clothing, and other necessities from local merchants. Accordingly the wives and children of ironworkers usually planted and cared for a garden; cooked meals; preserved food for the winter; spun and wove cloth; and made and repaired clothing.

ALL MEN ARE CREATED EQUAL
www.nps.gov/inde

Independence Hall is the birthplace of America. The Declaration of Independence and U.S. Constitution were both debated and signed inside this building. The legacy of the nation's founding documents - universal principles of freedom and democracy - has influenced lawmakers around the world and distinguished Independence Hall as a UNESCO World Heritage Site. Construction on the building started in 1732. Built to be the Pennsylvania State House, the building originally housed all three branches of Pennsylvania's colonial government. The Pennsylvania legislature loaned their Assembly Room out for the meetings of the Second Continental Congress and later, the Constitutional Convention. Here, George Washington was appointed Commander in Chief of the Continental Army in 1775, the Articles of Confederation were adopted in 1781, and Benjamin Franklin gazed upon the "Rising Sun" chair in 1787. The Declaration of Independence and U.S. Constitution were both signed in the Assembly room. Later, the room became a shrine to the founding of the nation, proudly displaying the Liberty Bell and original paintings of the Founding Fathers.

EGGPLANT PROVENÇALE

1 (1-pound) slender eggplant
1 very large tomato
2 tablespoons olive oil
fine sea salt
freshly ground black pepper
2 tablespoons bread crumbs
1 garlic clove, minced
1 tablespoon chopped fresh parsley
1 tablespoon olive oil

1. Preheat oven to 350 degrees.
2. With vegetable peeler, peel eggplant end to end. Cut in half lengthwise. Lay eggplant halves on cutting board flat sides down and slice in ⅓-inch slices.
3. Cut tomato in half. Lay flat sides on cutting board and slice thinly.
4. In a shallow baking dish, alternate eggplant and tomato slices. Pour olive oil over vegetables and season with sea salt and pepper to taste.
5. Bake uncovered until vegetables are almost tender, about 30 minutes.
6. In a small bowl, combine bread crumbs, garlic and parsley. Sprinkle mixture over eggplant and tomato. Drip remaining olive oil over crumbs. Return to oven until bread crumb topping is browned, about 3 minutes.

Serves 2 - 4

Recipes Index

INDEPENDENCE HALL

APPETIZER

Baked Crab, Lobster and Artichoke Dip 2
Chevre with Herbes de Provence 3
Coconut Shrimp with Mustard Sauce. 10
Crabmeat Stuffed Mushroom Caps 9
Cranberry Brie 7
Hot Mushroom Turnovers 11
Hot Oyster Spinach Dip. 3
Reuben Dip. 4
Sausage Stuffed Mushroom Caps 13
Shrimp Butter Toast 6
Shrimp Dip 8
Smoke Mullet Dip 5
Spinach Cheese Squares 12
Swedish Meatballs. 13
Tapenade Dip 4

APPLE

Apples and Butternut Squash 125
Apple Cranberry Pork Chop 63
Muffin 30
Scones with Maple Cream Sauce 25
Wild Rice with Apple 124

BANANA

Banana Cream. 98
Bread Pudding. 90
Muffin 24

BEEF

Chicken Fried Steak 70
Cranberry Short Ribs. 75
Marinated Beef Tenderloin 73

BEVERAGE

Cape Cod Cooler. 16
Mint Julep 17
Mojito 15
Raspberry Lemonade Cooler 14
Strawberry Sparkler 16
Sunset Sangria 18

BLUEBERRY

Johnny Cake 20
Lemon Bread. 21
Blueberry 96
Swirl Cheesecake 103

BREAD

Apple Scones with Maple Cream Sauce. 25
Blueberry Johnny Cake. 20
Blueberry Lemon Bread 21
Cranberry Apricot Scones 26
Date and Nut Bread 22
English Muffins. 28
Jordan Pond Popovers 27
Malbone House Spoonbread 23
Plantain 24

BREAKFAST/BRUNCH

Apple Frittata 36
Cheese Blintz 39
Crustless Asparagus Quiche. 40
Devonshire Eggs 34

Grand Marnier French Toast	35
Kuchen	38
Lemon Souffle Pancakes	35
Monticello Cheese Grits	37
Pannukakku	29
Sausage Puff	34

CAKE
Chocolate Praline Torte	91
Hummingbird	104
Smith Island 10 Layer	102

CHICKEN
Apricot-Glazed Rock Cornish Hens	69
Chicken Stoltzus	68
Orange Almond	64
Peach Stuffed Chicken Breasts	66
Southern Fried Chicken	67
Turkey and Cranberry Hash	71

CHOCOLATE
Bailey's Irish Cream Cheese Swirl Brownie	89
Candy Cane Brownies	88
Chocolate Praline Torte	91
Chocolate Walnut Pie	100

COOKIES
Bailey's Irish Cream Cheese Swirl Brownie	89
Candy Cane Brownies	88
Key Lime	93
Lemon Drop Cookies	91
Oatmeal Spice	93
President Kennedy's Lemon Butter Cookie	95
Rose Kennedy's Sugar Cookies	94

CRAB
Corn and Crab Bisque	45
Crab, Lobster and Artichoke Dip	2
Crabmeat Stuffed Mushroom Caps	13
Crab Scampi	78
Crab Crust Scrod	78
She Crab	42

CRANBERRY
Apple Pork Chop	63
Brie	7
Bran Muffin	32
Apricot Scones	26
Orange Marmalade	115
Short Ribs	75
Walnut and Blue Cheese	56

DESSERTS
Banana Bread Pudding	90
Blueberry Swirl Cheesecake	103
Chocolate Praline Torte	91
Coconut Rice Pudding	106
Lemon Tart with Berries	92
Maple Crème Brûlée	90

DIP
Baked Crab, Lobster and Artichoke Dip	2
Hot Oyster Spinach	3
Reuben	4

Shrimp 8
Smoke Mullet 5
Tapenade 4

DRESSING
Strawberry Vinegar 117
Warm Bacon 108

LEMON
Blueberry Bread 21
Butter Cookie 95
Drop Cookies 91
Souffle Pancakes 35
Tart with Berries 92

LOBSTER
Baked Crab, Lobster and Artichoke Dip 2
Popover 85
Stew 52

MUFFINS
Apple 30
Banana 24
Bran Cranberries 32
Dirt Bombs 33
Sweet Potato 31

PEACHES
Ginger 117
Low Country Peaches and Cream Pie 99

PIE
Banana Cream 98
Blueberry 96
Coconut Cream 97
Chocolate Walnut 100
Fried 101
Low Country Peaches and Cream 99

PORK
Apple Cranberry Pork Chop 63
Jaegerschnitzel 65
Roast Pork Loin with Orange Juice 64
Tropical Pork Chop 62
Sausage Stuffed Mushrooms 13

PRESERVES
Basic Pickling Syrup 110
Brandied Apricots 112
Calamondin Marmalade 112
Corn Relish 109
Cranberry Orange Marmalade 115
Ginger Peaches 117
Key Lime Curd 115
Mango Chutney 114
Red Onion Jam 113
Spiced Pumpkin and Pecan Butter 111

SALAD
1905 Salad 58
Broccoli Salad 55

Cranberry, Walnut and Blue Cheese 56
Marinated Cucumbers 60
Pineapple Pasta Primavera 57
Portobello Mushroom Scallop 59
Shrimp Salad 59
Strawberry Spinach 53
Waldorf 54

SANDWICH
Kentucky Hot Brown 72
Po Boy 79
Steak and Boursin 74

SAUCES
Cinnamon Hot Apple 118
Key Lime 116
Maple Cream 90
Mustard 116
Rémoulade 117
Strawberry Vinegar 117
Tarragon Vinegar 117

SEAFOOD
Broiled Cape Scallops 81
Coquille Saint Jacques 83
Crab Crusted Scrod 78
Crabmeat Scampi 78
Finnan Haddie 77
Grilled Striped Bass with Garlic and Basi 82
Haddock Chowder 44
Key Lime Baked Snapper 84

Linguini with Shrimp and Broccoli 86
Lobster Popover 85
Marinated Swordfish 76
Oyster Stew 49
Shrimp Po Boy 74
Steamed Mussels in Wine and Garlic 80
Swordfish and Pecans 77

SHRIMP
Butter Toast 6
Dip 8
Linguini with Shrimp and Broccoli 86
Po Boy 79
Salad 59

SOUP
Cheeseburger Chowder 51
Corn and Crab Bisque 45
English Cheddar Chowder 50
Haddock Chowder 44
Irish Potato Leek and Bacon 44
Lobster Stew 52
Navy Bean and Ham 46
Oyster Stew 49
Pasta y Fagioli 47
Potato with Bacon 49
Riesling Onion 48
She Crab 42

VEAL
Scallopini 75

Recipes Index

VEGETABLES

Apples and Butternut Squash 125
Asparagus with Honey Mustard Dressing 126
Baby Zucchini with Garlic Potatoes 121
Corn Souffle 127
Eggplant Provençale 128
Fried Green Tomatoes 122
Latkes 123
Rum-Glazed Carrots 126
Summer Ricotta Vegetable Tart 120
Tomato-Zucchini Tart 121
Warm Potato Salad with Bacon and Shallots 124
Wild Rice with Apple 124

COOKBOOKS FROM BASS POND PRESS

Send the completed order form with your payment to:
Bass Pond Press, 1305 S Branch Parkway, Springfield, MA 01129 U.S.A.

Taste and Tales of Our National Parks East
Over 150 recipes from across the country reflected of the region and 95 tales of many of our great National Parks...............**$18.95***

Taste and Tales of Massachusetts
Over 150 historical and fun tales from across the Commonwealth and 200 delicious and tasty recipes...**$19.95***

Taste and Tales of Cape Cod and the Islands
80 entertaining and informative tales; 150 irresistible recipes from the Inns, Restaurant, Bed & Breakfasts, and vintage cookbooks.
....**$16.95***

* Massachusetts residents add 6.25% sales tax.

Be sure to visit **tasteandtales.com** for more information or to order online or call 413-782-0924

ORDER FORM

Name ....

Address ....

....

....

Phone ....

Email ....

____ Taste and Tales of Our National Parks East @ $18.95/each

____ Taste and Tales of Massachusetts @ $19.95/each

____ Taste and Tales of Cape Cod and the Islands @ $16.95/each

____ A Taste of Cranberries and Some Tales Too... @ $12.95/each

____ Taste and Tales of Coastal New England @ $16.95/each

Note: Shipping cost is $5.50 per book. For credit card orders, shipping costs will be added to your total.

Order Total ....

Shipping cost $5.50 per book = ...

Total Enclosed ....

☐ Check enclosed (U.S. Funds only)
☐ VISA/MC

Card # ....

Name on Card ....

Billing Zip Code ....

Exp. Date .... Security Code ....

Signature ....

ORDER FORM

Name ....

Address ....

....

....

Phone ....

Email ....

____ Taste and Tales of Our National Parks East
@ $18.95/each

____ Taste and Tales of Massachusetts @ $19.95/each

____ Taste and Tales of Cape Cod and the Islands
@ $16.95/each

____ A Taste of Cranberries and Some Tales Too...
@ $12.95/each

____ Taste and Tales of Coastal New England @ $16.95/each

Note: Shipping cost is $5.50 per book. For credit card orders, shipping costs will be added to your total.

Order Total ....

Shipping cost $5.50 per book = ...

Total Enclosed ....

☐ Check enclosed (U.S. Funds only)
☐ VISA/MC

Card # ....

Name on Card ....

Billing Zip Code ....

Exp. Date .... Security Code ....

Signature ....

COOKBOOKS FROM BASS POND PRESS

Send the completed order form with your payment to:
Bass Pond Press, 1305 S Branch Parkway, Springfield, MA 01129 U.S.A.

A Taste of Cranberries and Some Tales Too...

Since the Pilgrims landed, cranberries have been enjoyed by generations of New Englanders. Enjoy over 80 recipes and 30 tales of the cranberry........................$12.95*

Taste and Tales of Coastal New England

75 interesting and historical tales from the Coast of New England and over 180 delectable recipes from the Inns, Restaurant, Bed & Breakfasts, and vintage cookbooks.
....$16.95*

* Massachusetts residents add 6.25% sales tax.

Be sure to visit **tasteandtales.com** for more information or to order online or call 413-782-0924